AVON VILLAGES

Avon Villages

EDMUND J. MASON
AND
DORRIEN MASON

PHOTOGRAPHS BY
JOHN H. BARRETT

ROBERT HALE · LONDON

© *Edmund J. Mason and Dorrien Mason 1982*
First published in Great Britain 1982

ISBN 0 7091 9585 0

Robert Hale Limited
Clerkenwell House
Clerkenwell Green
London EC1R 0HT

Photoset by
Kelly Typesetting Limited
Bradford-on-Avon, Wiltshire
and Printed in Great Britain by
Clarke, Doble & Brendon,
Plymouth, Devon
Bound by Western Book Company

Contents

Illustrations

PICTURE CREDITS

All illustrations are reproduced by kind permission of Mr J.
H. Barrett.

Acknowledgements

The authors wish to record their thanks and indebtedness to the many people who have supplied information for use in this book, with special thanks to the following:

Mr and Mrs J. Allen, Mrs Molly Ashley, Commander D. J. F. Atkins, Arthur Ball, Derek Boddy, Mrs Winifred Bush, the Reverend B. G. Carne, Commander and Mrs Katherine Christophers, T. J. Clayton, Wilfred Cocks, Alan Cole, Mrs Christopher David, Graham Davis, the Reverend K. F. Dimoline, Harry Dodds, Dr Zeta Eastes, Miss Jane Evans, Mrs Joy Gerrish, M. J. Gwyther, Mrs Anne Hore, Mrs Barbara Lowe, John Lucena, Michael Mapstone, the National Coal Board, A. H. S. Parsons, Miss Marjorie Pepperell, the Reverend John M. Prior, Mrs Mary Rowe, Mr and Mrs N. B. Sandiford, Mrs Pat Shales, W. C. H. Vowles, the Reverend A. F. Waker, Mrs S. Weatherill, Mike Winwood, J. P. Wynne Willson, and the officers and staff of the Avon County Council, Northavon District Council, Wansdyke District Council and Woodspring District Council.

1

The County of Avon

The County of Avon was formed in 1974, as the result of local government reorganization, from parts of North Somerset and South Gloucestershire and the City of Bristol which had been a county in its own right since 1373 by a charter of Edward III. For many years these areas had strong links with each other, for the inhabitants of North Somerset and South Gloucestershire had tended to look to Bristol, and, to a lesser extent to Bath, rather than to their own county towns, as the industrial, cultural and social centres. The new county was created amid the protests and petitions which usually herald changes. For months, car stickers were seen with the slogan "Save our Somerset" and many people refused to acknowledge that they lived in Avon, still heading their letters with "Somerset" or "Gloucestershire". Now, however, the controversy has at last died down and the county is assuming its separate identity in the eyes of the public, although people outside the West will sometimes ask: "Where is Avon?"

On the western side, the county adjoins the mouth of the River Severn and includes part of the estuary as far as the mid Bristol Channel islands of Steep and Flat Holms. The Mendip Hills, running from east to west, form a natural southern boundary, so that only villages on the northern slopes of the range are within the county. The combined towns of Radstock and Midsomer Norton, which have traditional ties with villages on the northern section of the old Somerset Coal Field and with the City of Bath, are also within the southern boundary. To the south-east of the county, the River Avon crosses the border between Wiltshire and Avon and, accompanied by the Kennet and Avon Canal, runs close to the eastern boundary, before sweeping westwards to enter Bath. North of Bath, the boundary runs through the Cotswolds on the line of the old border with Wiltshire, turning westwards north of Tresham. The northern boundary has no well-defined natural barrier until it reaches the River Severn, just north of the village of Hill.

The county is divided into six districts: Northavon to the north, Wansdyke to the east, Woodspring to the west, Kingswood adjoining east Bristol, and the cities of Bristol and Bath. The population of the county is just under 1,000,000, the greater part living in the highly populated areas of Bristol, Bath and to a lesser degree in Kingswood. The rest of the population is spread over the two hundred or more hamlets, villages and small country towns which occupy the much larger rural areas of the 520 square miles of the county.

For a county of comparatively small acreage, Avon has an astonishing variety of scenery, such as the gorges of the limestone hills, the drained marshlands bordering the Severn, the lakes of the Yeo and Chew Valleys and the steep Cotswold scarp. The geological formation not only shaped the countryside, but controlled the appearance of the villages. The grey limestone buildings of a Mendip settlement are easily distinguished from the mellow yellow stone villages round Bath, while the stone roofs of a Cotswold village contrast with the clay pantiles of the lowlands.

There is great variety, too, in architecture. Near the Somerset border, we find churches with tall, graceful towers, of a type known as Somerset towers, one hundred feet or more in height, often crowned by an elaboration of pinnacles. Although Avon is a county of church towers, there are some interesting spires, such as the almost unique spire of the church at Almondsbury. There are seventeenth-century manor houses, many still continuing their traditional role as farmhouses, and a wealth of Georgian buildings, from small dwellings fronting on to the village street, to fine houses in colourful gardens. Many of the larger houses, too big today to house a single family, have been turned into schools, hospitals, rest homes, offices, or divided into several dwellings. Although seventeenth-century and eighteenth-century buildings predominate, there are Tudor and even medieval houses and a great wealth of church architecture.

Avon is a county generally lacking in castles, for even the imposing mass of Thornbury Castle is really a castellated mansion, a memorial to the ill-fated Stafford, who left his mark on national history. However, there are several palatial mansions, such as Badminton, Dyrham, Dodington and Ashton Court, indicative of the wealth of the families who built them, who endowed our countryside with fascinating estate villages and enriched our churches. It is people who make history and not buildings and many of the men and women who lived in these mansions added much to Avon's history by their eventful lives. However, it was not only the great families who made the past interesting, but people who lived in more modest houses, like Hannah More and her sisters who set up schools among the miners of lead and calamine; and again, in their humble way, the miners, the craftsmen, the millers, the farmers and the fishermen have all contributed to our story.

The changes in Avon villages have mostly followed the general pattern in the rest of the country. In the inter-war years, the drift from the villages to the towns was accelerated by the agricultural depression and the increasing mechanization of farms, until today we are told that there is one man where, not long ago, twelve were employed and at some farms the big jobs are done by contract firms. In the church at Stanton Prior, a newspaper page of 1932 tells of the dramatic decline in village population. Cottages were cheap in the country villages and the rates hardly worth mentioning. Some friends had a nice little weekend cottage in Compton Martin for five shillings a week, less than a quarter of the town rent. This was for weekends, of course, for although the better-off people, from the Bristol merchants onwards, had often preferred a rural life, few urban workers wanted actually to live in the country.

If there was a movement from the villages in the early part of the century, there was certainly a movement back in the middle of the century, this time by townspeople. During the war, people were glad of a rest in the country from the Bristol bombing and perhaps this opened their eyes to the possibility of making their permanent home there, but in any case, as more and more people became car owners, more and more looked for a country home in peaceful, pleasant surroundings with large gardens. The empty cottages were renovated and modernized and the commuters came to live in the villages. The country folk had cars too and it was no longer necessary for them to move to the towns to work there. Today, it might be said that a country cottage is harder to find than a town house. Because of the compact nature of the county, these tendencies are particularly marked in Avon. Hardly anywhere is more than twenty miles or so from the city, so that every village is within commuter distance of Bristol or Bath.

There was once a world of difference between town and country. Beyond the Bristol tram and bus termini was the country, a place for workers on the land, with oil lamps and well water and privies at the bottom of the gardens. The villages themselves were reasonably self-contained, with their own shop, trades and crafts. The motor car has changed all that. Now the town dwellers drive into the country at weekends and on summer evenings and the villagers come into town for shopping, theatres and other amenities. The village shops lose their custom to the town supermarkets and, because so many families own cars, the rural bus services have become infrequent and expensive. These changes are hard on those without their own transport and, in some areas, private buses make the round of the villages on certain days to take the residents into town for shopping.

The village pub, the men's social centre, has often changed out of all recognition, from a place of stone-flag floors, old settles, shove-halfpenny boards and a great open fire, to fitted carpets, central heating, expensive decor and a variety of meals, serving not only local people but tourists from the towns. Where there is a bar for the local workers, it is often noisy with its juke box and Avon's traditional drink farmhouse cider, is hard to find.

Although the motorways have taken traffic away from certain main road villages on the A38 from Gloucester to Somerset, on the Bristol to Weston-super-Mare road and on the A4 to London, traffic through some other Avon villages has greatly increased, often with heavy vehicles thundering by and strings of cars, so that the peaceful scene has changed to one of noise and danger and it is safer for the old and young to walk on the city pavements than in the rural lanes.

All changes are not for the worst, however. The fading and decaying houses have been renovated and the villages are clean and neat, most of them taking a keen interest in the Best Kept Village competitions. There are plenty of activities, with clubs and societies, playgroups for the toddlers, church and chapel fêtes and pantomimes and, of course, full and interesting W. I. programmes. The new-comers usually enter into these activities with enthusiasm, although this varies from village to village. Generally, where the new-comers live in small estates or in individual old cottages and houses, they integrate well into the community, but where there are large new estates built on the outskirts, the new residents sometimes feel no part of the village and keep themselves apart from it.

In nearly all Avon villages, there is a strong interest in conservation and local history and there are many conservation bodies and local history societies, some arranging exhibitions and summer walks round their areas. The new residents are usually as keen as the older inhabitants to protect the best features of their village, the old buildings and the amenities of the countryside. After all, they have not moved into the country to see it spoilt.

Although mistakes were made in the past and some old buildings have fallen into a sad state of decay, modern legislation and planning attitudes have done much to keep Avon the attractive county it is today. Green belts occupy a large part of the county and most of the Cotswold and the Mendips within Avon are registered as areas of outstanding natural beauty. Industrial and housing developments are strictly controlled and only permitted in certain restricted areas. Some development is essential for the growth of any community and often conflicts with the desire to preserve our heritage, but the Avon Structure Plan has attempted to evaluate the development needs of the county commensurate with the need for conservation.

It may be interesting to speculate on the future, but because of so many unknown factors, predictions are uncertain. The motor car is largely responsible for the pattern of village life today, but what happens if the oil runs out? Already expensive petrol is producing some changes. In some villages trade is improving in the village shop. In others, residents are turning to the nearby small town or larger villages with shopping centres. Some people are thinking twice about moving too far from their employment. Are these signs of the times and will they change the village?

2

The Avon Valley

The River Avon enters the county close to Freshford, where it is joined by the Frome. The countryside here is typical of the whole area round Bath, an expanse of green low rolling hills, intersected by deep lanes, which suddenly open out into marvellous vistas, dotted here and there by a church tower or manor house. Here, we feel, is the serenity of the English countryside.

When Ealing Studios decided to make the film *The Titfield Thunderbolt* in 1952, they chose this area as its setting. The opening scene was taken at Freshford near the church, looking down the village street towards the old brewery. It is surprising how many old brewery buildings have survived in these villages.

You have only to go down to the medieval Freshford Bridge over the Frome, mentioned by Henry VIII's antiquary, John Leland, to feel the remoteness of this place from the hustle of nearby Bath. Near the bridge is The Inn which dates from Tudor times. It has no other name, but the emblem on its sign indicates its connection with the Methuen family, for the Methuens were the great landowners of this area. According to the landlord, in 1713 they added an upper floor to the inn which was then a dwelling.

The landlord told us that he had been at The Inn for seventeen years and when he first came there, Freshford was a close-knit village type community. The growing use of mechanized equipment meant that the many farm labourers had been replaced by a few farm "technicians" and many of the original villagers had left the community. He said that in the old days, there was a squire who understood the problems of the villagers and, being a magistrate, was often able to settle matters in or out of court. He lent his grounds for fêtes and was associated with village festivities. A number of houses had been occupied by the R.A.F., then by students of Bath University and, as the students moved on, the houses were being acquired by commuters from Bristol and Bath.

In spite of its changing residents, Freshford still remains outwardly the same, probably because it was the first village in the district to form a conservation area in accordance with the Town and Country Planning Acts. Its steep streets of predominating Georgian architecture form a harmonious whole, unspoilt by pseudo trimmings. The church lacks an imposing tower, but stands on high ground on the road junction, with the village sloping down on either side. Within the church is an array of wall tablets, including memorials to a family with the interesting surname of Bythesea.

Opposite the church is the early Georgian house "Ivythorpe" with a coat of arms on a "broken" pediment and pilasters of two different orders on the ground and first floors. Adjoining the church is the manor house, hidden away from the road, although a glimpse of it can be seen from the entrance drive. Below the church is a quaint building, The Old Parsonage, and at the bottom of the hill, facing the end of the road, is "Avondale" with a fine doorway. When we last saw the house it was occupied by Bath students. To one side of it is the old mill-like building, once a brewery, with its tall slender chimney. The older parts are of early Victorian origin. It was at Freshford that Sir William Napier, the great campaigner and probably the greatest of our military historians, completed his history of the Peninsular War.

To the north of Freshford, the road runs out of Avon and into Wiltshire for a short distance, but enters the county again south of the Dundas aqueduct, an imposing structure of 1804, which took the Kennet and Avon Canal over the River Avon. Although this section still contains water, it has not been navigable for some years. Part of the Kennet and Avon Canal has been restored by voluntary labour for the use of present-day narrow boat and cruising enthusiasts and no doubt this section will be improved in due course. You can still walk along the tow-path and there is a way down to the bank of the River Avon.

Adjoining the aqueduct there is a bend in the canal's course, with a wharf and derrick still intact and one or two small buildings, relics of the trade which once went on there. At this point was the junction with the Somerset Coal Canal, con-

structed in the early nineteenth century to transport coal from the
Somerset coalfield. It has long since been filled in but its route
and the tops of its stone-built sides can still be seen in the garden
of the adjoining house. For enthusiasts of industrial history, quite
a few remnants of the old canal system can be found in the
woodlands of this area, which because of various levels once
incorporated some of the most intricate engineering feats of canal
construction.

A short distance west of the Dundas aqueduct and on a tributary of the River Avon, the Midford Brook, is Monkton Combe. It
is well known for its public school. In the nineteenth century, a
local clergyman started a small school for training the sons of
missionaries and from this humble beginning developed the
public school for boys we see today. The school occupies a long
string of buildings of various dates which front the main road of
the village. The oldest is a fine house in seventeenth-century
style, although it bears the date of 1714. Modern additions to the
school have been made adjacent to these buildings.

Close to the school is the inn, the "Wheelwright Arms", an
attractive but peculiarly shaped building, almost flat iron in form,
with its narrowest face to the road. Further along towards the
church, a rather ugly Victorian building of the Gothic style of the
period with a saddle roof, is the old brewery and malthouse.
These and adjoining buildings have been well converted into a
pleasant quadrangle of dwellings. The main brewery building
has been divided into flats and the loading bay leads to lock-up
garages. We think this is one of the most satisfying estate conversions we have seen and one which does not detract from the
appearance of the village.

As at Freshford, life in the village has changed, largely because
of farm mechanization and the car. With Bath two miles away and
Bristol within striking distance, it now houses many residents of
the commuter class. According to one local resident, it not only
has a commuter section of the community, but the school
provides an academic element and neither are fully integrated
into village life. Another resident in the area told me that the
depopulation of farm workers was not the only agricultural
problem. The laws protecting farm tenants made him loath to let
a farm for normal farming purposes, so he let the land for
pasture, a bad agricultural policy, he said, as it put nothing back
into the land, while he had converted the farmhouse into flats for
townspeople.

About half a mile from Monkton Combe is Tucking Mill. It is a hamlet consisting of only a few houses, but on one of them a plaque reads "Here lived William Smith, father of English geology, born 23rd March 1769, died 28th August 1839". The occupier told me that Smith actually lived at the next house in the trees, adjoining the lane to Monkton Combe, but the plaque remains in spite of attempts to have it moved. Smith, who laid down the principles of rock stratification and identification by fossil contents and who earned the nickname of "Strata Smith", lived at Tucking Mill for only a short time, from 1796-7. This was a temporary residence, his home being in Bath.

Smith was appointed engineer for the construction of the Somerset Coal Canal in 1794 and during the previous year, he had been engaged on the survey for the canal. He was born in Oxfordshire and died at Northampton. Today there is no tucking mill, only a house of that name.

Claverton is another attractive village, just outside Bath's boundary, on the western slope of the Avon Valley. The village is a single street of charming stone houses, some as old as the seventeenth century. There are just a few modern houses, conspicuous at the moment because of their new reconstituted stone, but no doubt in time this will weather to the golden mellow hue of the old stonework.

Along the village street is a wide space, enclosed by a balustrade of carved stone and an iron gate. Behind the gate are the overgrown terraces of the garden of the old manor house of Claverton, which was built in 1588 and badly damaged during the Civil War. It is said that the lord of the manor, Sir William Bassett, and his friends were disturbed at dinner by a cannon ball falling into the dining-room. Skirmishing took place in Claverton and the surrounding area and three parliamentary and one royalist soldier were killed near the ferry and buried by the west wall of the local churchyard.

The most important monument in the churchyard is the mausoleum of Ralph Allen, who became postmaster of Bath. According to some sources, he gained this position by finding letters in the post about a proposed Jacobite rebellion. He carried out a number of postal reforms, grew rich on the proceeds and embarked on the successful exploitation of Bath stone on his estate. He used it for his Bath mansion, Prior Park, designed by John Wood the Elder. There he entertained many famous people, including Alexander Pope, the "Wicked asp of Twickenham".

Allen had an eye for business, and the local oolite we call Bath stone became popular in Bath and further afield. He was elected Mayor of Bath in 1742 and did a great deal for the improvement of the city. He died in 1762 at the age of seventy-one and is buried under an imposing monument with other members of his family. It consists of a large box tomb, approached by three steps, surmounted by a roof, supported by arches.

In 1820, a new manor was built on the hill above Claverton, using some of the stone from the old manor house. It was designed by Sir Jeffry Wyatville in classical style and now houses the popular American Museum, the first of its kind outside America.

The village street runs close and parallel to the busy Bath to Warminster road, which takes all the through traffic, so that the village is unusually quiet and peaceful. On the other side of the main road, the land slopes down to the canal and the river, a pleasant spot in which to enjoy the beauty of this section of the Avon Valley. The conspicuous mansion on the slope on the opposite side of the river is Warleigh Manor now a school.

Bathampton is to the north of Claverton, on the Kennet and Avon Canal, where the church, the George Inn and the canal provide a delightful setting. The "George" can be entered either from the road or from the canal tow-path. This part of the canal is navigable. The inn dates back to the seventeenth century or perhaps earlier and, although there are modern extensions, they are in stone and do not detract from the inn's ancient look. Here, in the latter part of the eighteenth century, Viscount du Barry, nephew of Louis XV's mistress, was brought mortally wounded in the last legal duel, although not the last duel, to be fought in this country. He had quarrelled with his friend, Colonel Rice, and they had fought it out on Bathampton Down, overlooking the village. The viscount was buried in the local churchyard and is said to haunt the inn.

In a way, Bathampton is a place of pilgrimage, not to the viscount's grave, but of Australians to the burial place within the church of the first Governor of New South Wales, who had carried out the initial colonization of Australia, Admiral Arthur Phillip. His grave remained in obscurity until in 1891 authorities in Australia began to make enquiries about his burial place and traced it to Bathampton. The gravestone was renewed, but in 1967 the Vicar, the Reverend Gordon Spencer, appealed to Australia for a more suitable memorial and the result of this appeal was the memorial to Admiral Phillip's memory which we now see in the church. An existing chapel, which contains memorials to members of Ralph Allen's family, was converted to the "Australian Chapel".

We wonder how many of us, as children, looked forward to a box of Harbutt's modelling plasticine clay among our Christmas presents? Their factory can be seen on the other side of the canal from the tow-path near the inn.

After crossing one of those bridges that are rare today, a toll bridge, we reach Batheaston. Above rises Little Solsbury Hill crowned by a triangular hill fort, one of the earliest Iron Age hill forts in the country. It is the simplest of hill forts, surrounded by a low bank on which once stood a palisade.

The oldest part of Batheaston is at North End, where the church is to be found, a Victorian reconstruction, with the exception of the fifteenth-century tower and a font dating from about 1700. The more interesting houses and cottages are opposite and further up the street. One of the most imposing houses on the same side as the church is Eagle House, so named because of the large stone eagle perched on the pediment of the gable adjoining the road. With outstretched wings, it looks ready to swoop down at any moment. Under it is the date 1725. The house was built for his own occupation by John Wood the Elder, one of the great architects of Bath. Like several of the larger houses in Batheaston, Eagle House is built with its gable end to the road. The drive and courtyard now give access to several modern houses, built in what was once the extensive grounds of the house. From 1882 to 1962, Eagle House was the home of the Blathwayt family and Mary, the daughter of Colonel Blathwayt, was a well-known suffragette. On the opposite side of the road is a fine three-storeyed old building with triple gables and to the south a smaller double gabled house.

Batheaston, like many villages, is a mixture of old stone buildings and modern reconstituted stone houses which will need a lot of mellowing before they blend with the older dwellings. However, the good proportion of the older houses in Batheaston enables the village to retain its character. On the western outskirts of the village is Batheaston Villa, built in the late eighteenth, century for Sir John and Lady Miller. Lady Miller was a poetess and held amateur poetry contests there.

East of Bath is Bathford, where the church and even the tower date from Victorian times, but with some older work, including a

Norman doorway, which some say may be a copy, a thirteenth-century font, a Jacobean pulpit, finely carved with the inscription "Blessed are they that hear the word of God and keep it", and the old village stocks in the porch.

As the name implies, there was an ancient ford here, across the Box Brook, not far from its junction with the River Avon. The ford was replaced by a stone bridge. The steep streets, with some fine Georgian houses, climb the slopes of Bathford Hill from where there is a good view of the Avon Valley, Bathampton, some of the terraces of Bath, Batheaston and the flat top of Little Solsbury Hill. Around the church are other impressive eighteenth-century houses, including another Eagle House, a little younger than the one at Batheaston, but still designed by John Wood the Elder. Some way along the ridge above Bathford is Brown's Folly. After the Napoleonic Wars, there was the usual economic depression with attendant unemployment and Mr Wade Brown, a local quarry owner, had the tower built to give employment to local labour.

West of Bath is Newton St Loe, named after the St Loe or de Sancto Laudo family, named in turn after St Lo in Normandy. This family once held the manor at Newton St Loe and also the manor of nearby Corston. On the left of the road leading to the church is the old school house, now a private residence. Over the door, an inscription tells us that originally it was a free school built and endowed by Richard Jones of Stowey in Somerset and dated 1698. Opposite is a house dated 1715 with a porch surmounted by a pediment with a fossil ammonite at its centre.

The oldest and most interesting parts of the church, the south porch and aisle, are fourteenth century, but it suffered the usual nineteenth-century reconstruction. Just inside the door are the vault and monument of Joseph Langton who bought the manor of Newton and of his grandson, Joseph, who built the present house in Newton Park, and members of their family. In the vault are buried no fewer than eight children of the elder Joseph, including the son and heir, Joseph, who died aged twenty-four in 1701. On the magnificent monument, a heart-rending inscription records the tragedy of youthful mortality common to the era and the despair of the parents as death followed death. Three children died very young and three survived only to early adulthood. The inscription is in Latin, but a translation has been fastened to a nearby column. The impressive monument is enclosed by a railing, probably the earliest example of cast-iron work in the south-west of England. Unfortunately, it has no gates, which must make cleaning difficult.

Much newer wrought-iron gates in the village lead into the grounds of Newton Park, now a college of further education. It is one of the most impressive eighteenth-century mansions in the county. It was built by the second Joseph Langton in the early 1760s and it has recently been established that the architect was Stiff Leadbetter. The two wives of Joseph are buried in the family vault: Charlotte, who died in 1757, and Bridget, who died in 1774, so it was probably built on the occasion of his marriage to Bridget.

In the grounds is a thirteenth-century keep, used in more recent years as a library. Occupied as a residence for some centuries, the keep has undergone alterations and extensions, but the original form is still discernible. When we visited it in 1979, students were excavating the area adjoining the keep in search of the limits of the old manor house. Close to the keep and probably dating a couple of centuries later, is a fine gatehouse. There is a range of old buildings and some modern college buildings have been erected in other parts of the grounds, which were originally laid out by "Capability" Brown.

With an eye to extending the family estates, the second Joseph purchased the neighbouring manor of Corston. Here the Bristol-born poet Robert Southey went to a school run by a Mr Flower at the manor house. The house is still there at the bottom of a lane leading off the main road a short way past the church. It is a surprise to come upon this fine house, with its long façade and splendid shell-hooded doorway, in this out of the way place, surrounded by farm buildings. It was clear from Southey's "Retrospect" that the school was not all it purported to be:

> Methinks even now the interview I see,
> The mistress's glad smile, the master's glee;
> Much of my future happiness they said,
> Much of the easy life the scholars led,
> The best instruction and the tenderest care;
> And when I followed to the garden door
> My father, till through tears I saw no more,
> How civilly they sooth'd my parting pain,
> And never did they speak so civilly again.

It seems that young Southey spent a miserable time at Corston, not only at school, but in Corston church, for he wrote:

I saw the church where I had slept away
The tedious service of the summer day:
Or listening sad to all the preacher told,
In winter waked and shivered with the cold

The thirteenth-century nave and chancel of the church have been much restored, with the north aisle added in the second half of the nineteenth century. The tower is dated 1622, but is much restored. In the chancel are memorial wall tablets to the Harington family, who held Corston manor before the Langtons.

On the other side of the River Avon is Kelston, with its conspicuous feature, the tree-crowned Kelston Round Hill, known locally as Kelston Tump, a landmark which can be seen for miles around. Kelston is a pleasant little village on a main road to the north of the river from Bristol to Bath. Adjoining the village is Kelston Park, a house not so impressive as Newton Park, but a pleasant Georgian dwelling with an excellent view of Newton St Loe from its terrace overlooking the river. It was built by John Wood the Younger about 1770, for Sir Caesar Hawkins, a surgeon to George II and George III. The estate eventually passed to a branch of the Inigo Jones family. Kelston Park is now used by the Methodist Association of Youth Clubs as a Residential Training Centre.

The house replaced an earlier manor house, damaged in the Civil War and long since demolished. The site of the old manor is said to be adjoining the church in the village. At that house lived Sir John Harington, a godson of Elizabeth I. Tradition has it that he related an indiscreet story to her ladies. Queen Elizabeth was not amused and he was ordered back to Kelston. He was in disgrace on a number of occasions, once for making an allusion to the Earl of Leicester in one of his many writings. He accompanied Essex in the Irish campaign and annoyed the queen by receiving his knighthood in the field. His subsequent writings about the campaign aroused the royal anger and contributed to Essex's downfall. However, Harington outlived Elizabeth and died at Kelston in 1612. The old manor house was graced by Elizabeth in 1591, but entertaining royalty was an expensive business and Sir John Harington was forced to sell St Catherine's Manor to pay his debts.

Like many churches, that at Kelston was rebuilt in the latter half of the nineteenth century, but contains a few ancient pieces including a part of a Saxon cross. In the churchyard, against the wall, is the grave of the Inigo Jones family of Kelston Park.

Opposite the church is Manor Farm with an impressive ancient porched barn and adjoining it is an old and exquisite dovecote, square in shape with a remarkable number of nesting holes. Nearby is a row of fine old buildings. On the main road is the "Crown", an eighteenth-century inn, where the old court was held. The miniature beer engine is said to be the oldest of its kind in the country and beer is still drawn from it. Kelston holds another record. On a bend on the same road, is "Tower House" or the "Towers", built about 1850 with its curious tower and in its garden is reported to be the oldest flush toilet in the country.

On the river bank is the old eighteenth-century Kelston brass mill, its two tall annealing towers conspicuous from the "Jolly Sailor" across the river. Because of available water power, brass battery mills developed along the Avon from the 1720s onwards and places such as Kelston, Saltford and Keynsham thrived on brass industry until the last battery mill closed at Saltford in 1908, no longer able to compete with Birmingham, although the factory was still rolling brass up to 1925.

The old brass mill at Saltford is by the weir and adjoins the road known as the "Shallows". It is now part of a boat yard serving many of the pleasure craft that use the Avon and moor in the vicinity of the Kelston Lock. A low tiled roof building, it stands in a picturesque setting on an island close to the bank.

Skilled brassworkers from the Netherlands were brought over to assist in the manufacturing processes of the brass works and many of their descendants still live in the area of Saltford and Keynsham. The mills on the Avon had a world-wide clientèle, which included India and America. The American trade was by far the most important and when eventually the United States began to develop their own brass industry, the local industry suffered severely, not only from loss of trade, but because its skilled workers were attracted to the American mills. These factors, together with the growing competition from Birmingham put an end to the Avon brass industry.

The battery process consisted of hammering out brass by huge mechanical hammers and the din from these was enormous. It is said that Handel wrote his "Hallelujah Chorus" as a result of hearing the rhythm of the hammers at the mill at Saltford although some claim this honour for the Keynsham brass mill. The Shallows were once part of the stagecoach route from Bath to Keynsham and for those who enjoy riverside walks, this is one of the most pleasant areas of Saltford. They should also go along to the Saltford Lock by the Jolly Sailor Inn, which was once a stopping place for commercial barge traffic on the Avon.

In the early eighteenth century, locks were erected and the river made navigable from Bath to Hanham and so to Bristol. In December 1727, the first barge, loaded with iron and wood, made the complete trip between the two cities. Advantages to some often mean disadvantages to others and barges brought coal from Shropshire by the Rivers Severn and Avon to the disadvantage of the local coalminers. They retaliated by breaking down the Saltford Lock. Damaging the navigation works carried the death penalty, but the rioters were lucky, for none was caught. Barges were hauled by manpower until the nineteenth century, when the introduction of horse barges brought problems, for there were no continuous tow-paths. The horse had to be transferred to the other bank at intervals by means of horse ferries, wide, flat-bottomed boats, pulled across the river by a chain. There was one by the Saltford Lock where the tow-path changes banks.

The "Jolly Sailor" provided not only refreshment and accommodation for the bargees, but stabling for the horses. The inn still retains a curious memento of those days, for the wood surround of the fireplace in the bar has numerous holes. It was a tradition of the barge crews that when one of their number was promoted to master, he had to bore a hole with a hot poker and put down money for drinks for all present. Over the fireplace is a painting dated 1726, showing the "Jolly Sailor" and a former lock.

As we walk up to the village, we come to another public house, the "Bird in Hand". While the "Jolly Sailor" catered for the bargees, the "Bird in Hand" became an inn in 1869 to serve the men engaged on the Midland Railway. The G. W. R. line was laid earlier in the 1830s, through a tunnel which runs under Tunnel House higher up the village at the junction of High Street and Norman Street.

If we continue up High Street from the "Bird in Hand", past old stone-built cottages, we come to Queen Square, a name more imposing than the site, for it is just the wide entrance of a lane, adjoining the school and leading only to the church and the manor house. The church could not be more basic in its interior design, but with a certain charm of simplicity. There is little doubt that the original church was Norman, of the same period as the manor house, and remains of this work are seen in the tower and in the beautiful and unusual font, with eight heads carved round its octagonal base. Some authorities put the font as early as the

Saxon period and some as late as the thirteenth century. As a compromise, we wondered whether the bowl of the font, which looks Norman, could be older than the elaborately carved base.

In the porch is a most curious gravestone giving the story of the unfortunate Frances Flood, whose legs are buried in the church-yard. She arrived in Saltford when she was thirty-two in 1723, when a sick and penniless stranger could not expect a welcome in any village. Since the overseer could not help her, she found shelter in a pigsty and then a roofless barn. Even then the owner removed the door. She was shown some kindness for she was sent food and drink, but otherwise she had no attention for fourteen days, when her legs began to turn black and the flesh fall away. The overseer brought her some ointment, but after some weeks, her left leg broke off below the calf. She dressed the wound and it healed, but eventually she lost the other leg. She attributed her recovery to divine intervention, but it is a great wonder she survived to leave her legs behind in the churchyard.

The manor house adjoining the church is one of the oldest dwellings in Britain. The front which faces you from the gate is seventeenth century, but the original house was Norman and some features survive from this period including a window on the north face, together with early Tudor work. Exceptionally interesting items are the wall paintings on an upper floor, believed to be of twelfth and thirteenth-century date and at one end of the roof ridge you can see a huge carved figure of a crouching lion.

Norman Road leads up to the main Bristol to Bath road, where modern and between-the-wars housing appears. To many people who travel along A4 road, this ribbon development is Saltford and it is in fact part of modern Saltford only, while the old village runs down towards the river. The expansion of Saltford and its neighbour Keynsham is such that only a small rural strip separates them.

Keynsham lies between the confluence of the Rivers Avon and Chew. It is not a village, but a small country town, although there is so much of a village atmosphere about it that many of the inhabitants refer to it as a village. Situated between Bristol and Bath, it is now partly a dormitory area for Avon's two cities, but most of the commuters live in the extensive housing estates on the outskirts and in the centre there is still a good sprinkling of old Keynsham among the modern shop fronts.

Ancient Keynsham was the settlement which grew up round

the great abbey which crowned the high land behind Station Road, between the Rivers Avon and Chew. It was founded by a charter dated 1171, made by William, Count of Gloucester, in accordance with the wish of his dying son, Robert. Dedicated to the Blessed Mary, St Peter and St Paul, it was one of six Augustinian establishments in Britain, with St Victor in Paris as their mother church. All were in the West Country and three of them were in Avon, being Keynsham Abbey, Woodspring Priory and St Augustine's Abbey, the forerunner of Bristol Cathedral.

Part of the foundations of Keynsham Abbey were uncovered during the building of houses in Abbey Park in 1865 and a portion remains standing in the garden of the terminal house at the far end of the west side of Abbey Park. In 1961, Mr Mervyn Samuel drew the attention of the Bristol Folk House Archaeological Society to the fact that "Abbotsford", then threatened by construction of the impending bypass, probably stood on part of the Abbey site. With myself as Director of excavations, the Society undertook the excavation of the "Abbotsford" site, the line of the bypass and, later, part of the park adjoining the bypass. As a result, the greater part of the outline of the Abbey church, the cloisters and adjoining buildings have been revealed.

In common with other religious houses, Keynsham Abbey was dissolved by Henry VIII in 1539, peacefully in this case. The abbot was pensioned off, the great buildings dismantled and the materials sold.

It would be nice to think that the origins of Keynsham go back to St Keyna or Cenau, although the modern name of Keynsham and its Domesday Book name of Canesham may owe their origins to a tribal name. St Cenau was one of a number of children of Brychan, the freckled one, chief of Breconshire. Young and beautiful, she fled from her many suitors across the Severn and travelled up the Avon to seek a quiet place in the shelter of the wooded valley. The local chieftain gave her a plot of land for her cell, but he was not so generous as he appeared, for the land had no "development value", being infested by snakes. These creatures were no problem to St Cenau, who turned them into stone by the power of prayer. You can still see them about Keynsham today, the coiled fossil sea shells called "ammonites". There is still a living species of ammonite today, the pearly nautilus. Finally St Cenau died at Keynsham in a blaze of light and her body was taken back across the Severn to Wales.

There now appears little doubt that there was a Saxon

establishment at Keynsham because of the Saxon material found during our excavations and the Saxon carved stone embedded in the back of the archway in Station Road, which, although thought at one time to be part of a Saxon cross, is believed by Dr Basil Cottle and myself to be part of a Saxon grave slab.

Keynsham's history goes back beyond St Cenau's time, the fifth century, for there were several Roman villas in the area. One of the largest in the county is under Keynsham cemetery on the Bristol road. It caused much trouble to the gravedigger who complained of "bumping" through old walls. A smaller villa was found when digging foundations for Fry's chocolate and cocoa factory, now part of the Cadbury-Schweppes complex at Somerdale. This villa has been removed to just within the factory gates. Finds from both villas and some material from Keynsham Abbey have been housed in a small museum nearby. It seems to have been quite a populous area in Roman times, for remains of other villas have been found at Newton St Loe, Burnett and Brislington, and the Roman baths at Bath are not far away.

The parish church of St John the Baptist, at the corner of High Street and Station Road, was restored in the nineteenth century, but still retains its thirteenth-century chancel. The ledger or grave slabs in the south porch were removed from the Abbey site during excavations and placed there for safe keeping. The largest, that of Hugo Taylour and Matilda, his wife, and children, probably benefactors of Keynsham Abbey, was too big to fit into the porch and is outside between the two buttresses adjoining the porch. It once rested in a central position just within the west door of the former Abbey church. There is within the church an elaborate monument to Sir Henry Bridges, who died in 1587, and another to Sir Thomas Bridges, who died in 1661.

On the south side of Station Road is a quaint archway incorporating fragments of Abbey stone. This is said to be a doorway to the vanished mansion of the Bridges family and has been rebuilt on the present site. After the Dissolution, the ruined Abbey must have been a quarry for building stone and decorative carvings. These, with the ammonites, can be seen inset in buildings in many places in Keynsham and in the front of one of the old houses on the north side of Station Road, fragments of stone and a medieval tile from Keynsham Abbey have been inserted. A medallion carved with a figure of a sheep in the wall of an old public house, "The Crown" on the Bristol road could be a boss from the Abbey or an emblem of the wool trade. Higher up the road is an archway with a strange mixture of stone fragments and some, including a fragment of Saxon-style carving, appear to be from the Abbey.

Next door is a strange contrast between old and new. A Tudor house with stone mullion windows sits snugly behind a garage forecourt, with the modern garage adjoining. The forecourt has been raised several times and the tiled gabled roofs are now almost at eye-level. Below and on the same side of the road are the Bridges Almshouses, a gift of Sir Thomas Bridges in the seventeenth century, with two shields bearing the arms of his family. The almshouses became unfit for their purpose and the interior has been converted into two private dwellings.

At the top of Bristol Road, opposite the modern flats, is the seventeenth-century Manor House, with its low porch and short tower. Next is High Street, the hub of the town, with its modern shops, although if you look above the ground-floor level, you will see many evidences of seventeenth- eighteenth-century Keynsham and here and there a real gem still exists.

From the twelfth to sixteenth century, Keynsham was dominated at its northern end by the tower of Keynsham Abbey and now the skyline is dominated at the southern end of High Street by the modern Civic Centre, which, like the flats, is the object of disapproval among some residents, a disapproval often aroused by modern architecture. Although opinions vary about the appearance of the Centre, few can question its convenience, for here the housewife can park her car, do her shopping, pay her gas bill, make her complaints to the Council, change her library book and enjoy the sports centre and the view across the Chew.

3

Kingswood and the Forest

From Keynsham, it is only a short distance across the River Avon to Bitton on the upper Bath to Bristol road. The River Boyd, the source of water power once for several mills, passes Bitton on its way to join the Avon just south of the village. The string of buildings along the main road gives little clue to the attractive part of the village that lies to the south near this junction. Church Road turns off the main road at the early eighteenth-century White Hart Inn and leads past the old buildings belonging to Church Farm, probably the site of the manor house. Further down the road is the church with its great Somerset-type tower, although Somerset was once just across the river. The building goes back to Saxon times and there are still some traces of Saxon work in its fabric. It has been suggested that there may have been a Romano-British church here because of Roman remains found in the churchyard.

As we entered through the north vestibule and the fine Norman doorway, probably not in its original position, into the north-west corner of the nave, we were astonished at the size of the church. It was built on this scale to serve a much larger area than at present. My eye was caught by the fine hammer-beam roof with its gilded angels and unusual pierced filling of the spandrels which was erected in 1867 from wood from a shipwreck in the Bristol Channel. The pews were made by local craftsmen in the 1870s, while the woodwork of the old pews was used in the ceilings of the Dower House. No transepts remain, but on the site of the north transept is the Lady Chapel, built by Bishop Thomas de Bitton of Exeter in 1299 as a chantry chapel, and standing in a corner are two stone coffins with worn effigies, found on the site of the south transept in the Grange garden. They are thought to belong to Sir Robert de Button and his wife Emmote de Hastings, the bishop's parents.

To the left of the altar are two adjoining ledger stones of the two Seymour brothers who lived at the Grange. One was a murderer and the other his victim. On 30th January 1742, Berkeley Seymour sold some cattle in Bristol and returned to the Grange with the money, where William shot and robbed him. William galloped off towards Gloucester, but stopped for attention to his horse's shoes and paid the smith with a guinea of the stolen money. This guinea happened to have a hole in it and was subsequently identified to convict William, who was hanged at Gloucester. His body was returned to Bitton for burial in the church and some years ago it was noticed that one of the grave slabs had been steadily rising. However, this was not being pushed up by an unquiet spirit, but by the steady growth of a tree root.

The church is not without its ghost. Mrs Joy Gerrish, the local historian to whom I am indebted for much of the information about Bitton, told me that her grandmother, while arranging flowers in the church at the beginning of the century, saw a woman in grey near the choir vestry making in the direction of the Grange. The figure was one of no mortal substance and Mrs Gerrish's grandmother fled. The ghost was not seen again until the Second World War years. Then an occupant of the Grange was mending his bicycle just inside a door when a woman, whom he assumed to be his wife, quickly passed him. When his wife assured him that she had not left her chair in the lounge, the old story came to mind.

Vicars come and go and may soon be forgotten, but two are not. They were the Ellacombes, father and son, who between them were vicars of Bitton for ninety-nine years. The earlier H. T. Ellacombe is probably best known for the Ellacombe chimes, a mechanical bell-ringing system he invented. His apparatus is still in use at Bitton church and it was, of course, the first church to be fitted with the chimes. They are played at different times to those of the bell ringers, but if the ringers should ever fail to turn up, the chimes can always be operated.

In 1952, I was asked to examine some human bones uncovered, during excavations for a new sewer, between Church Road and the churchyard wall. Three skeletons were eventually found.

Freshford as seen from the church

Old Brewery, now converted into flats, Monkton Combe

Canal Terrace, Kennet and Avon Canal, Bathampton

Newton Park, Newton St Loe

The Old Brass Mill, Saltford

A Tudor house, Keynsham

Manor house and church, Bitton

Narrow boat moored on River Avon, Hanham Mill

Sally on the Barn, Court Farm, Hanham Abbots

Syston Court

Statue of Neptune, Warmley House

Old cottages, Aust

Disused jetty of the former Aust to Beachley ferry

Jacobean staircase, Elberton Manor

Manorial pew in St Michael's Church, Hill

One was that of a muscular man about thirty-five years of age at death and showed traces of arthritis. The other skeletons were those of a woman and probably a child. They were orientated in Christian fashion and were doubtless a family group grave. There were no signs of coffins and the bones could not be dated. The churchyard wall had been re-aligned in 1850 for road widening, but records dating back to 1600 showed no burials in that area. These burials appear to have been made before coffins were general and the teeth wear showed grit in the diet usually due to the use of hand mills, so they could easily have been pre-1600 burials.

South of the church is the Grange, formerly the rectory and originally the prebendary manor house. It is the central and largest house of a charming group of stone buildings. They are now separate dwellings and known as the Grange, the Dower House, Granchen and Grange Cottage, separated from the road by a ha-ha. The Seymours lived in the Grange and over the door is their emblem, the joined bird wings. John Wood the Younger lived there in the eighteenth century and made extensive alterations. He was a churchwarden at Bitton from 1760 to 1765.

Granchen, as its name implies, was the Grange kitchen and has one of the largest fire openings I have ever seen. There is a suggestion that the cellars of Granchen may have been used for salting meat for the winter and as the brewery.

As in many other well-preserved villages, there are but few people who work on the land in this elegant backwater. The residents are mostly commuters to Bristol and Bath, including a large proportion of professional people, keen to maintain a quiet village atmosphere and conserve its old buildings. They have been threatened by national large-scale developers but, in spite of pressure and public inquiries, the Parish Council, aided by the planning authorities, have won the day and retained the village identity here, so different from the area to the north of the main road, where housing and other development have all but destroyed the rural character of the place.

On the south side of the Bristol to Bath road are still traces of old Bitton. One is the Constable's House which had a barred room at the rear as a lock-up. The two houses adjoining were once a workhouse on the ground floor and a pin factory on the first floor. The redundant railway station at Bitton is now used as a Railway Centre for the public display of old locomotives and railway stock and the operation of steam engines.

On the Bath road on the east side of Bitton, we come to the cluster of buildings by the river which is Swineford or Swinford, which owes its name to the legend of Bladud, a prince reluctantly banished by his father because he was a leper. He got a job as a swineherd at Keynsham, but the pigs contracted his complaint. Fearing the wrath of his employer he drove the swine across the river at the shallows which then existed at Swineford. By some instinct the pigs rushed towards Bath and into a morass, where the mud cured their leprosy. Bladud took the same cure with spectacular success and subsequently built baths over the curative springs for which Bath became famous. There were copper mills at Swineford and the complex of buildings dating from the 1840s still remains with two undershot waterwheels.

On the Bristol side of Bitton at the junction with the Bristol to Bath road and the road to Keynsham is the hamlet of Willsbridge and up the hill in the direction of Bristol, a castellated house stands high up on the left-hand side of the road. This is Willsbridge House known also as Willsbridge Castle because of its battlements which were added in the nineteenth century. It was once the home of the Pearsalls and one of them, Robert Lucas Pearsall, was a famous composer of madrigals, and songs such as "Oh, Who will o'er the Downs so free?" It is said that at Willsbridge House, Pearsall would sit at his piano composing his pieces with a cat tucked into the top of his dressing-gown.

The Pearsalls were great landowners and industrialists in the area. In the eighteenth century, one member of the family, John Pearsall, built an iron rolling and slitting mill on the reputed site of the old manor house. It can be seen from the opposite side of the road to Willsbridge House and approached by a footpath. It is a large three-storeyed building with a loading bay, loading doors on each floor and a mill pond at the rear. In 1816, its use changed to that of a flour mill and later for the manufacture of pig food, but in 1968, the building was put out of action by the disastrous floods which swept away bridges at Keynsham and Pensford. In 1979 the building, windowless and a shell, was presented to the Kingswood District Council, who propose to restore and adapt it as an amenities centre.

A footpath, railed and embanked above the valley, follows the stream up to Oldland church. The path was brought up to its present state under the Jobs Creation Scheme and it makes a pleasant walk, with a good view of the valley below. Presently the path crosses a lane and a great stone-built embankment comes into view across the valley. This embankment carried the tramway to Willsbridge and Londonderry Wharf on the Avon and the lane was a gravity-operated incline to bring coal from the California Colliery to connect with the tramway. The mine closed in 1904 and was one of the last to be closed in the Kingswood Forest.

Close to Willsbridge, the old tramway passes through a tunnel and when I visited it some years ago, it was used for mushroom growing. It was used as an air-raid shelter during the raids on Bristol in the last war. People, with suitcases and blankets, used to arrive from the city and camp for the night in the tunnel. One of the local clergy would visit them and sometimes hold a service. The water company now use the tunnel as a convenient pipe route.

The footpath soon reaches the cluster of grey stone cottages near the stream and the hillock on which is perched the church of St Anne at Oldland. One of the dwellings was once a bone mill where bone buttons and other articles were made. The church stands on the site of a much older building. It was built in 1830 and the adjoining vicarage was built twenty years later to form a pleasant complex on the hill overlooking Oldland Bottom. Many churches were built or restored during the nineteenth century, for in 1820, Parliament voted a million pounds towards church building in industrial areas, in an attempt to combat the social unrest following the industrial revolution and the growing popularity of the nonconformist churches.

Today, Oldland and the surrounding area is mainly a commuter district, with some farming and industry here and there, but in the nineteenth century, industry was very much to the fore. There were the miners from California Colliery and other pits, while many of the inhabitants were engaged in boot and shoe-making, one of the principal industries of Kingswood and the surrounding district. There was employment in the mill at Willsbridge and there was the ancient felt and beaver or fur hat-making occupation, until the fashion for silk top hats was introduced in the middle of the century.

The main village of Oldland is on the higher land at Oldland Common, where there has been much modern development with so many new-comers that it has been generally difficult to preserve the village identity. An elderly inhabitant told me that in the old days everyone knew each other and he could leave a pound note on the path through Oldland Bottom on a Saturday and pick it up again on a Monday. I don't know whether he had actually ever tried it.

We return to Willsbridge and on to Longwell Green, with its new housing estates. Here there is a plastic factory and a coachworks. The coachworks used to make carts and wagons and went on to make bodies for mechanized vehicles, including those for buses, lorries, fire engines and crane cabs. Their products are internationally known.

From Longwell Green, we can get down to the River Avon at Hanham Mills, with its riverside public house, the "Chequers". It has been well modernized, with extensive car parks, but at least the outside of the original part has not changed since the time it served the bargees of the Avon. Adjoining the "Chequers" and facing the river, is a string of cottages and a house, known as the old bakery, which might well have been connected with a mill. On a small island close to the river bank are the walls of an old building with some arches and, between the island and the bank, is a deep slot of water which may have been a waterwheel housing. Remains of further walls were exposed in 1979, while clearing debris for a private garage for use with one of the cottages. This site is believed to be that of a former brass mill.

The narrow hill leads up from the "Chequers" towards Hanham Abbots and by turning right around a small triangular green and right again, we find ourselves on a gravel drive leading to the church and to Hanham Court. You cannot find one and miss the other because the church tower is attached to a wing of Hanham Court. The church is mainly fourteenth century, with a fifteenth-century tower, but suffered two restorations, one in the nineteenth century and one in the early twentieth. Inside it is white and bare, devoid of monuments, but there is a fine Norman font and thirteenth-century piscina, probably both from Keynsham Abbey, for the manor of Hanham Abbots for over two hundred years belonged to the Abbots of Keynsham, whose Abbey stood on the other side of the river. The manor was surrendered to the Crown with Keynsham Abbey and its numerous other properties at the Dissolution. The last abbot, John Stourton, was awarded a very handsome pension for his peaceful surrender, but there is a story that, in the presence of his canons, he stood on an adjacent hill at Hanham Abbots and pronounced a solemn curse on the despoilers of his favourite estate.

Hanham Court is an interesting sixteenth- and seventeenth-century house with some later work and is believed to be on the site of the older manor house which existed in the time of Keynsham Abbey. After the Dissolution, the manor passed into various hands and in 1638 was acquired by the Creswicke family, who occupied it for two hundred years.

Perhaps the most colourful member of the family was Francis, who married the daughter of a London alderman. There was bad feeling between Creswicke of West Hanham or Hanham Abbots and the Newtons of Barr's Court, of East Hanham, over manorial rights. The Newtons lost the case, but were to get their revenge. In 1685, Francis Creswicke heard that Monmouth had reached the area with his rebel army and was encamped in a meadow opposite Keynsham. Anxious about two stacks of hay which he owned in the vicinity and curious to see the rebels, he set out for their camp. Unfortunately, he was recognized by a Captain Tylie of the rebel troops, who rode out to greet him and the incident was reported to his enemy, Newton. Much of Creswicke's hay had been used by Monmouth's supporters and Newton was able to make the accusation that Creswicke had collaborated with the rebels and sold them hay for twenty guineas.

Following the defeat of Monmouth's army a few days later, Creswicke was arrested for treason and jailed in Gloucester awaiting trial, which was continually delayed by Newton's tactics. Through Creswicke's wife's connections, a plea was eventually made to the King who ordered enquiries and when Monmouth's chief officers confirmed that Francis had no part in the rebellion, he was released after six months in Gloucester Prison. His pardon was complete, for in 1686, we find him entertaining the King and his company at Hanham Court, an entertainment which meant raising a mortgage on the Court.

Francis Creswicke could not manage to keep out of prison for in 1704, he wounded the Attorney General, of all people, in a quarrel in Dublin which sent him to prison for nine years. On his release, his creditors had him back in prison for debt, but he survived to live to the good age of eighty-nine. He died in 1732 and was buried in the churchyard at Bitton.

The Creswickes triumphed over the Newtons in the end, because although Hanham Court has survived, the only visible evidence of the Newtons' manor house, Barr's Court, between Longwell Green and Cadbury Heath, is a moat which still holds water, but Leland's "fayre old mannar place of stone" has long since gone.

Adjoining Hanham Court is an ancient tithe barn, probably of the fifteenth century, with a two-storeyed porch with a pyramidal roof. Another interesting barn, although of later date, is at Court Farm about a quarter of a mile away. It is known as "Sally on the Barn" because of the stone female figure on the roof. There is the usual story of "Sally" coming down from her perch at midnight, but it is generally accepted that the figure is one of Ceres, the corn goddess.

On the Bristol road through Hanham is the "Blue Bowl" public house, the oldest public house in Hanham and one of the oldest in Britain. It is even claimed that it was a wine shop for the Roman legions, but be that as it may, it was certainly mentioned by St Lyte in 1480 as an established hostelry. Cromwellian troops were billeted there in 1645 *en route* for Bristol. No doubt over the centuries it has been a meeting place for nefarious characters, for it was at the Kingswood Chase, a lawless place, that wild miners encroached on the forest for coal and timber for props poaching and looting. They formed themselves into gangs and the most formidable was the Cock Road Gang who met at the "Blue Bowl" in the early eighteenth century. Their leader was Richard Bryant who, it is is said, slept at the inn always with his boots on, ready to make a quick getaway. One day, he wasn't quite quick enough and was arrested and hanged in Bristol for the murder of his father. Later in the eighteenth century, the British bare-fist champion, Jim Belcher, lived at the "Blue Bowl". He finally lost his title to John Cribb, another Hanham man who never lost a fight.

Two religious groups attempted to bring the gospel and a little education to these rough miners of the forest. The Baptists preached to them for some twenty-six years in the seventeenth century and had to contend, not only with the miners, but with persecution from the authorities. In the eighteenth century, George Whitfield and John Wesley began their open-air preaching on Hanham Mount, this time with considerable success. Many joined their ranks and there was even a watch-night service on Saturday nights to lure the miners away from the taverns. Wesley founded a school at Kingswood and some of the ignorance and lawlessness gradually disappeared from the area. The open-air site on Hanham Mount can still be visited, although the surroundings are much more built up than when we first knew it.

A high metal beacon was erected in 1951 to mark the site and at night its green light can be seen for miles around. The beacon is approached from Mount Hill Road across a modern paved courtyard and then by a circular flight of steps. On the approach of the steps, a bronze plaque let into the wall shows a preacher holding up a bible with the inscription: "From 1658-1684 persecuted Bristol Baptists preached in Hanham Woods to the people of the neighbourhood. The preachers often swam the flooded Avon and risked imprisonment and death for their faith". From the base of the beacon, a footpath leads along the ridge of the Mount to a wooden pulpit, a replica of that used by Wesley in his Kingswood school. Round the base are inscribed the words, "All the world is my parish". In the forecourt beneath the mount, a plaque tells us that George Whitfield and John Wesley preached their earliest open-air sermons on the mount in 1739 and gives some extracts from both their journals recording these occasions.

There is another well-known memorial in Hanham and that is in Memorial Road itself. In 1876, John Chiddy noticed a large stone in the path of an express train and managed to remove it from the line, thus averting a serious accident. Sadly, he was killed doing so and a cottage, known as Memorial Cottage, was erected for his family by public subscription. The well-built little house, a very practical expression of appreciation, still stands in Memorial Road, near Memorial Close. There is a plaque recording the incident on the flank wall.

From a dip in the Bath to Bristol road, Troopers' Hill Road leads down to the River Avon. There is a good deal of recent housing development at the top of the hill, but a picturesque part of Hanham lies at the bottom at Crews' Hole. It is said that Bristol sailors used to come up the river to hide here from the press gangs and there are the usual rumours of smuggling. Climbing up the hill is an interesting network of lanes with old cottages, some modernized, but with one or two cottage-type pubs. The area retains its character. A little way down the river is a tar works which used to distribute its products by barge traffic.

A little way up the river is Conham Ferry. The small boat is kept on the opposite side at Bees Tea Gardens, a favourite stopping place for the pleasure boats plying to and from Bristol. The chances are that one of the dogs in the garden will bark and someone will call out asking if you want the ferry. This was one of the number of ferries which used to cross the Avon, once the only means of communication between the settlements on the two banks.

Like a number of places in the Forest, Hanham once had its collieries and metal works and today there are several mostly light industries, as indeed there are round the north and east borders of Bristol.

There is little in the north of Hanham to distinguish it from the large urban spread of Kingswood and there is little at first sight to distinguish Kingswood from the larger spread of Bristol. There is no mistaking the origin of Kingswood's name, for the ancient royal forest stretched right across Kingswood. A forest in this sense did not mean merely woodland, but included scrub and open heathland. There was a royal forest here in Saxon times and the royal Saxon hunting preserves were taken over by the Norman kings. The ancient boundaries cannot be traced precisely, but at one time the forest seems to have covered a considerable area of the county from the River Severn to the River Avon, including what is now part of east Bristol.

Like all forests, its boundaries must have varied from time to time and its area gradually diminished until in 1228, Henry III granted a charter of disafforestation, converting much of the forest to common land, but retaining a small royal "chase". The Constable of Bristol was responsible for the Forest and employed four verderers on behalf of the king, each with their own territory, but when his supervision ended in the seventeenth century, encroachments increased and the forest laws became more and more inoperative. Illegal wood cutting, pasturing of animals and mining of coal in the forest became common. Encroachments or "liberties", involving possession of the land itself, did much to destroy the chase. After 1662 new wardens were appointed, and in the eighteenth century, the royal rights became obsolete. There are several commons in the area, such as Syston Common, which may be the remnants of the chase. The coal mining which did so much to exterminate the forest was a feature of Kingswood until the middle of the nineteenth century and George Whitfield and John Wesley did much to improve the spiritual and mental state of the miners.

Kingswood today is such an urban area that it is indistinguishable from its contiguous neighbour, Bristol, and there is no green belt to separate them. Much of the development took place in the eighteenth and nineteenth centuries when cottage industries such as shoe and pin making were common in the area, to be eventually replaced by industrial establishments. Sometimes small factories, served by cottage industries grew enormously, such as Britton's boot and shoe works. Sometimes small factories supplying larger industries developed other lines and became independent concerns. An example was the Douglas motor cycle works at Kingswood.

William Douglas came to Bristol in 1882, as a repairer of shoe and boot machines. He and his brother set up a factory at Kingswood, to make shoe lasts, lamp posts and other iron products. William's son became fascinated with the early development of motor engines and met J. J. Barter who had developed the Fee light motor cycle, one of the earliest motor cycles in Britain. Eventually Douglas reluctantly took over the production of the "Douglas" motor cycle with Barter as production manager, In 1907 the Douglas motor cycle came into being and in 1914 a heavier machine capable of taking a sidecar was, again reluctantly, brought out by Douglas. During the 1914-18 war, the War Department ordered huge quantities of motor cycles for dispatch riding and Douglas produced 25,000 machines, a great contrast to the time when William Douglas repaired boot machinery and made shoe lasts. The company made their last cycle in 1954 and was eventually absorbed by the Westinghouse Brake and Signal Company.

King's Chase, Kingswood, an appropriately named shopping complex, opened in 1975, included the site of the surgery of Dr E. M. Grace, a brother of Dr W. G. Grace. Like his brother he played cricket for England and Gloucestershire on many occasions. After the complex opened, occupants of three shops on the surgery site reported that they heard ghostly noises and experienced strange happenings, such as the mysterious switching on and off of an electric kettle, disturbance of their display goods and the sound of footsteps up the stairs, followed by the flushing of the toilet.

Northwards are the built-up areas of Soundwell and Staple Hill, where there was a small pin factory. Near Staple Hill is Mangotsfield on the edge of the built-up area. The manor house once adjoined the church, In fact, it was a little too close, as the house and its land were acquired in 1846 for the enlargement of the churchyard.

In monastic times, the church of St James was a chapel of ease to St Peter's Church, Bristol, and both belonged to the Priory of St James, Bristol. It was much restored in the nineteenth century and at the end of the century was the scene of the extraordinary Shipway Fraud. Mr R. W. Shipway, living in Chiswick, engaged a man named Herbert Davies to trace his family tree. Today this is a favourite hobby of our classless society, but in the nineteenth century, the establishment of a pedigree was essential to the newly rich, anxious to take a place in society. One of the lines of enquiry by "Dr Davies", as he called himself, concentrated on Mangotsfield church, where he found ample evidence of his client's ancestry. This evidence was fraudulent. It included an inscription, dated 1541 on a belfry beam, which had not been installed until 1687. There were six entries in the parish registers concerning the Shipways, although the duplicate registers contained no such entries and Shipway inscriptions were found on the ancient plaster of the chantry and on a tomb in the nave. In fact, the name of Shipway had suddenly appeared in all directions. Davies even claimed that a stone statue dug up in the chantry in 1896 was one of the Shipways. Accounts of the discoveries appeared in local newspapers of 1896, but by 1898, the fraud was exposed and Davies sentenced to a three-year term of hard labour. You won't find any trace of the fraud in the church today as the Bishop ordered all the "evidence" to be removed and the forged entries to be erased.

An interesting house is Rodway Hill House on Rodway Common, once a manor house of the Berkeleys. It is a three-storeyed house with skewed chimneys and stone Tudor window frames with typical hood moulds. Anne Boleyn may have visited this house when she came with Henry VIII to visit Bristol, as Lady Anne Berkeley who lived in the house was a friend of the royal family.

Between Mangotsfield and Frenchay and within the heavily built-up area is Downend. There is very little trace of the old village where iron used to be worked and it is a long time since the whipping post and stocks stood in front of the "Green Dragon". The derivation of the name is not so simple as it seems and may have originated in the family name of the Downings. Downend was the birthplace of Dr W. G. Grace in 1848, that indefatigable cricketer, who played for England when he was only eighteen.

To the east of Mangotsfield is Pucklechurch, a name which conjures up visions of elves and fairies, although it has been suggested that the origin of "puckle" could be a word meaning beauty or even a word meaning a stack of corn. We do know, however, that the Saxon King Edmund had his palace or hunting lodge here in the royal forest. In 946, on St Augustine's Day, the king was feasting with his retainers at the palace when he was stabbed to death by Leolf, an outlaw whom he had banished six years earlier. The king was buried at Glastonbury, where he had installed St Dunstan as abbot. There is no trace of the royal palace today, but it was probably made of timber as were most Saxon palaces.

In 1185, the people of Pucklechurch were fined forty shillings for causing "waste". Under the forest laws people were allowed certain privileges, such as lopping trees in the appropriate season and any damage beyond the established privileges was "waste".

Situated on the edge of the Bristol fringe urban development, Pucklechurch has more of a village atmosphere than those nearer the city and administratively it is outside the Kingswood District. Although there is quite a lot of new development, it is nicely spaced out and at the heart of the village, round the thirteenth-century church, there are still a number of grey stone cottages and fine seventeenth-century houses, connected with the Dennis family, such as the "Grey House", which is thought to have been the family Dower House, and Dennisworth Farm. There is a spacious thirteenth-century church with monuments of the Dennis family, who lived in the Grey House and at Dyrham and who built Syston Court.

This imposing sixteenth-century mansion is at the village of Syston or Siston, south west of Pucklechurch. From the road, it is best seen when coming from the south. At a bend in the road, the house comes into view on the left, perched in a commanding position on the ridge. The lodges on either side of the entrance drive, in spite of their old world look, are in fact of the nineteenth century. Syston Court is now divided into several units and these make very pleasant dwellings while retaining the character of the Tudor mansion.

When we visited the house some years ago, the central part was occupied by the Women's Land Army. One of their tractors had sunk into what was thought to be an underground passage on the south side of the house and we were asked to investigate. It was a square box-shaped tunnel of flat stones, so low that we had to stoop. We crawled northwards towards the house, only to find that the square tunnel rapidly diminished, making further progress impossible. It was, in fact, a rainwater drain. Before underground pipes were common, a convenient way was to trench and build up the walls and sides with slabs and this meant that the trench had to be large enough to work in it, except where it was tapered to take the rainwater from the downpipes. Many an old drain or well overflow has been mistaken for a secret underground passage.

The magnificent oriel window, on the east wall of the north wing, which faces us as we come up the drive, is said to be the window from which the young lady of the Dennis family, locked in her room, escaped to join her lover, Hickory Stern, and to ride "o'er the Downs so free", as Pearsall's song puts it. The house, which is built round the three sides of a court, is made even more conspicuous by its two corner octagonal towers, surmounted by ogee roofs and ball finials. Among the famous people reputed to have visited Syston Court was Oliver Cromwell, who is said to have left a pair of boots there in 1642.

Just down the road from the Court is the church of St Anne. Cromwell may have left his boots at Syston Court, but his troops left their bullets in the oak door of the church and carried out other destruction, such as the damage to the water stoup inside the porch. It is a moot point which is worst, the damage done by Cromwell or some of the alterations to our churches in the nineteenth century. Syston church, although restored in 1887, still has its Norman nave and an exquisite Norman doorway. Over the door, the tympanum is carved with the tree of life and the supporting columns of the door arch are covered with carvings, each column different from the other.

The church is the proud possessor of a rare font, one made completely of lead. There are less than forty lead fonts in England and the one at Syston is the only example in Avon. The figures round the sides look Saxon, but the font is Norman. The wall paintings in the chancel and on the chancel arch are the early twentieth-century work of two ladies of the Rawlins family who lived at Syston Court. The church still has its eighteenth-century manorial box pew and seventeenth-century oak pulpit. The churchyard walls have been topped with the slag coping stones, so familiar in the district and were probably made at the old spelter works at Warmley. The tiny village is charmingly rural with ancient farm buildings and a sprinkling of modern houses leading down to a stream.

South-west of Syston is Warmley, just within the edge of the developed Kingswood area. It once had the largest brass and copper works in the world, established by William Champion in 1746 to develop his process for making zinc or spelter from calamine which was mined on Mendip. For a long time, calamine had been used for making brass, but Champion found that, by reducing it to zinc, the manufacture of brass could be reduced in cost. Champion patented his invention in 1758, but in 1779, James Emerson, a manager at Warmley, set up his own works at Hanham, where he patented a new process which produced brighter coloured brass. This is the same method used today. Copper is the other ingredient for brass making and Champion had copper mills. The round tower still standing on the old works site is believed to have been part of one of these mills and to have given the factory its name of Tower Works.

Overlooking the works, Champion built himself a fine house, Warmley House, now used as offices by the Kingswood District Council. He laid out the grounds with a summer house, paths, shrubberies and trees and constructed a large lake, not only for ornamental purposes, but to provide a head of water for the mills. On a small island in the centre of the lake, he erected an enormous statue of Neptune, made of slag from his works. What is left of Neptune has been partly cleared of ivy in recent times and the huge monolith with the legs of the sea god can be reached through the trailer park. Over the brook which ran from the lake, Champion built an arch and over the arch erected a castellated structure as a residence for his groundsman. This building still exists, flanked by two modern extensions which do not altogether harmonize with the old buildings. The black quoin stones were made of slag from the works. This slag was also made into coping stones and blocks and can be seen in buildings and walls for miles around the area, including his pseudo-medieval castle at Arnos Vale. Looking out from the terrace of Warmley House, it is difficult to imagine these pleasure grounds as they were in Champion's time, for most of the drained lake site is now filled with the residential caravans of the Kingswood Trailer Park.

Of the works themselves, with the exception of the old round mill tower, some broken walls and a few odd pieces of machinery about the grounds, all that is left is a three-storeyed building with a corner clock tower, a conspicuous feature seen from the road. After the works came to an end, the factory site was used by Haskins Potteries for pipe making and after that enterprise closed down, the clock tower building was occupied by an organization called "Slab". A tablet on the wall states that the building, erected in 1743, was opened for Slab as an experimental arts and community centre by Mr Selwyn Lloyd in 1973. It is now thought that the building is rather later than the date shown on the plaque.

"Slab" closed in 1978 and the building is now used by the

Clocktower Association as a centre where young adults not only have leisure facilities, but are offered opportunities to improve their skills. The association is an independent voluntary organization depending on grants, donations and particularly on voluntary participation. It has done exceptionally good work in assisting unemployed school leavers and spina bifida young people.

The old factory area at the back and on one side of the building has been developed into a small industrial estate of modern factories, producing goods of various kinds.

Like the rest of the Kingswood district, Warmley was once a coal mining area and from these local mines, Champion obtained the fuel he needed for his furnaces. Originally on the coach road from Bristol to London, it has some old houses, but now mostly nineteenth-century cottages, with the inevitable modern development, although it retains the character common to villages with early industry.

4

Severnside

To the west lies the City of Bristol and through the city runs the River Avon on its way to join the Severn in the Bristol Channel. The north bank of the Avon is within the Bristol boundary, but beyond the north western outskirts of the city lie the lands bordering the River Severn, low-lying pastures, once marsh land, but now traversed by drainage channels. Here and there are areas of higher ground with village settlements and ever-recurring views of the Severn, with the hills of Gwent and the Forest of Dean beyond.

The first villages reached from Bristol along Cribbs Causeway are the twin villages of Compton Greenfield and Easter Compton. Easter Compton is the main settlement, strung out along the road to Pilning, but the old houses and church are at Compton Greenfield, scattered among the lanes a short distance to the west. The church still has its fourteenth-century tower and a magnificent late Norman doorway with three orders of elaborate mouldings and delightful serpent head stops. Inside is a fine well-pointed transitional chancel arch and tablets to the Davis family who lived in the early nineteenth-century Hollywood Tower, now used as the headquarters of a milk distribution firm. For a hundred years between 1170 and 1270, this small church was served by clergy from the ecclesiastical college at Westbury-on-Trym. From 1671 to 1683, the rector was Samuel Crossman, who wrote the hymns "Jerusalem on High" and "My Song is Love Unknown". Not far away is the sixteenth- to seventeenth-century manor farmhouse with its tall mill-like appearance.

A group of small children with their teacher came along to the

church while we were there and we were invited to visit their
school, a red-brick, gable-ended building in the main road at
Easter Compton. When we arrived, the children were sitting at
small tables enjoying their school dinners, while we spent a
pleasant half hour examining their charming drawings pinned
round the walls of the single classroom.

The name Compton is said to be derived from "combe", a West
Country word meaning a valley, and "ton", a settlement, while
Greenfield refers to the family name of former lords of the manor,
the Grenvilles. The land is not entirely agricultural. The Bristol
and Clifton West of England Zoological Society own quite a large
area, where they keep some of their animals, grow some of their
animal feed and cultivate flowers for their zoological gardens.
Cider apple orchards are also a feature of the district.

The development of Easter Compton, away from the church
and along the Pilning road, was largely the result of the construction, between 1873 and 1886, of the Severn Tunnel. The building
of this railway link between England and South Wales brought a
great influx of people to the whole area round Pilning and Severn
Beach, including Cornish miners and many craftsmen. Houses
were enlarged and others built cheaply to accommodate them,
transforming the district, which until then had been quiet marshlands with a scattering of fishermen's cottages and farmhouses.
Indeed, Pilning itself was probably named after one of these
farms, Pilning Farm, now Fox Farm, while the River Severn
provided the area's most important occupation, that of salmon
fishing.

Severn Beach became popular as a picnic area in the early years
of this century. Wealthy families came down in horse brakes to
spend a day on the pebbly beach by the Severn. Mrs Mary Rowe
told us that her great grandparents, Mark and Hester Britton,
lived in a house on the sea bank and when Hester was asked the
name of the shore, replied, "The beach by the Severn—Severn
Beach". The place grew popular as the destination of a "day out"
and the next generation of Brittons served teas to the visitors and
another member of the family sold water at 6d a glass. With the
passenger halt in 1922 and the station in 1926, Severn Beach grew
rapidly. The railway ran excursions and evening trips and
hundreds of people came to the little resort. A swimming-pool
was built and part of the sea wall laid out as a promenade.
Gradually, however, the boom came to an end. The motor car
widened the horizon of the masses and they no longer flocked to

Severn Beach on the cheap railway excursions. Nevertheless the walk along the sea wall with fine views of the Severn is very pleasant and, as new estates are built, many people are finding Severn Beach an agreeable place in which to live and commute to Bristol and Avonmouth.

The old villages of the area are a mile or two further north, Northwick and Redwick, originally remote villages of the marshes, which were gradually drained by the rhines or "pills" as they are known locally. The sluice gates are tide operated. Where each pill reaches the estuary, there are great sluice gates and the rising tide shuts these gates and prevents flooding of the pastures by the salt estuary water. When the tide recedes, the fresh drainage water opens them and allows the land to drain. Mr Arthur Ball, Chairman of the Parish Council, told us that the people living in the area have to pay drainage rates, which they feel is unfair because the water flows from the higher ground where people do not have to pay these charges.

Northwick itself is a tiny village with some pretty old houses, particularly Church Farm, near the church which was built in 1840 with several others in the living of Henbury. Northwick church fell into decay and was eventually pulled down, but the churchyard cemetery still exists and the impressive tower in neo-Romanesque style was purchased by the parish council and preserved as a Severnside landmark. Adjoining the church is the school, now Redwick and Northwick School, but originally Sandford's Charity School, founded in 1781 by Robert Sandford, who left a legacy so that poor country children might be taught to read and write.

Redwick itself is a straggling hamlet on the way to New Passage with some old houses. A pleasant way to New Passage is to walk along the sea wall, the Binn wall, from Severn Beach. Here the Severn estuary becomes the Bristol Channel with the second greatest rise and fall of tidal water in the world, so this well-kept wall with its clean solid masonry is very necessary. We walked along to New Passage one January day. This was the favourite walk for trippers to Severn Beach in its heyday because at the New Passage hotel was the nearest public bar. The estuary gleamed in the winter sun as we passed Salmon Pool, a long stretch of deep water between the rocks, English Lake further out and then stretch after stretch of The English Stones where during the Civil War sixty Parliamentary troopers were drowned by a trick of the ferrymen. Charles I and his royalist force had been ferried across the Channel from the Black Rock at Portskewett by loyal boatmen, who returned to the Welsh shore to find pursuing Parliamentary troops demanding a passage. The ferrymen tried to delay them with excuses about the state of the tide, but the troopers insisted on a passage. The boatmen steered for The English Stones, which from that side of the Channel and at low tide appear to run to the English shore. They told the troopers that it was usual to alight on the stones and scramble over them to the shore, but when the boats had departed, the Parliamentarians found deep water lay between them and the shore. The tide rose with such a speed that, laden with armour and equipment, the whole party were soon drowned. Needless to say, Cromwell was furious with the ferrymen and closed the ferry, which did not operate again for nearly a century.

Past these outcrops in the Channel we come to New Passage, where coach passengers and later train passengers embarked on the ferry for South Wales. A fine hotel, now demolished, was built here and even a hospital for the convenience of passengers. Smart new dwellings, with fine views of the Severn, surround the site. Ahead is Aust and the Severn Bridge, appearing so fine and attenuated that it might be a toy erection over which pass mechanical cars.

Just before the Severn Bridge is the site of Old Passage, first a ford and then a ferry across the Severn from early times. It may have been this way that the Bishops of the Celtic Church came to meet St Augustine in A.D. 603. Aust would seem an obvious meeting place and indeed it is said that the name of the village is derived from that of the saint, although there are other possible origins. Bede does not give the site of the meeting place, except that it was near the border of the Huicci and the West Saxons. Some claim the honour for College Green, Bristol. St Augustine arranged the meeting in an attempt to unify the Celtic Church with that of Rome, but it was unsuccessful because St Augustine did not rise to greet them and, offended, they departed.

In recent times, there was a boat ferry for cars and foot passengers. The *Severn King*, the *Severn Queen* and the *Severn Princess* worked in pairs, leaving Aust and Beachley more or less simultaneously. Often we have waited for the ferry at Old Passage to save the sixty-mile road journey via Gloucester, only to be told there were no more crossings that day due to the tide. The car jetty was a rickety affair, but it is still to be seen today with the grass growing up between its rotting boards, boards that used to rattle as we drove down to the hinged gangway on to the boat. Foot passengers could cross for a shilling and there was a special day ticket for a shilling return.

The old ticket office and café are now frontless and the rest of the building is gradually rotting away. The abandoned toilets at the end of the building still have their turnstile, the tall variety, rather like a revolving cage, which moved when you put your penny in the slot and you felt you ran the risk of being inextricably trapped. Surely this must now be an item of industrial history. With the 470-foot-high towers of the Severn Bridge, looming skywards, and its 3,240 feet of road span, suspended by what looked like mere wires from our position by the jetty, we have here an example of the old boat ferries superseded by the great road bridges of today. One wonders whether those great structures will, in turn, suffer the same fate.

Adjoining the jetty and between the Severn and the old ferry approach road is a broad greensward, wet in flood conditions but reasonably hard at other times. Its tufty character makes it difficult to believe that here was once run the Waterloo Races. Part of it is now used as archery butts.

Overlooking the old ferry is the brown stucco-faced Old Passage House, once an inn for coach passengers and drovers before they embarked on the ferry. The Irish cattle drovers once slept in the attics on their way to and from Bristol market. Now the house is a private dwelling.

The main part of Aust village is cut off from the Severn by the new carriageway to the Severn Bridge. You have to cross this busy road to get to the church and the only surviving pub of the many village inns, the "Boar's Head". It is an old building and was certainly there in 1729 and was probably an ale house before that. It was once a staging post on the journey to Wales. The fact that this was the last village before the ferry crossing made Aust, with its inns, an important place for lodging and refreshment. The railway diminished the importance of the village, but it was still a useful place for road travellers until the construction of the Severn Bridge. Now what was once the road to London is a cul-de-sac sealed off by the new motorway. Without the traffic which once rumbled through its street, Aust is now a quiet backwater and what it has lost in business, it has made up in peace and tranquillity, with its rows of old cottages and little new development.

The church, mostly of the fourteenth and fifteenth centuries, stands on a rise to the west of the village. This too has a connection with the crossing, for in the corner between the left wall of the porch and the tower, as we approach the church doorway, is the communal grave of several victims of ferry boat disasters. Much of the wording has flaked off, but some of the carved words are still distinguishable.

The cliffs at Aust, with their various coloured strata and examples of faulting, are geological hunting grounds, particularly the Rhaetic bone bed, famous for fossils of prehistoric reptiles. Here we once had the good fortune to come across a tooth of an ichthyosaurus, or so we were assured by a local geologist.

A short distance east of Aust is Elberton with its church dedicated to St John. It has a fourteenth-century tower, but much of the church was restored in 1858 and again in 1900. An interesting feature is the Jacobean manorial box pew, with carved panelling and four holes for inserting sprigs of holly at Christmas time. On exhibition are three ancient bibles, the oldest being a Black Letter Bible of 1613 and a Basket Bible of 1721.

The relationship of church to manor house is still apparent for a door from the churchyard leads into the garden of the manor. The sixteenth- to seventeenth-century house is a tall, three-gabled, grey stone building, with a cupola on its roof which, no doubt, would have given the previous owners a good view of their labourers working in the fields. On the flank wall of the house is a housing for a bell, probably used for calling in these labourers when the house was a manor farmhouse. The fine barn and other farm buildings are now a separate holding.

One of the most famous farmers born at the manor was Joseph Sturge, Quaker, philanthropist and agitator against slavery. He was born at Elberton Manor in 1793 and attended a day school at Thornbury and later boarded at the Sidcot Quaker School. Although he made much of his fortune as a corn chandler, he refused to sell barley to breweries. He also refused to pay fines for not joining the militia and many of his sheep were taken in lieu. When he was twenty-nine, he moved to Birmingham, where he became Secretary of the Birmingham Anti-Slavery Society. He even went to the West Indies to prove that he could grow sugar without slave labour, and after the abolition of slavery, he fought for the education and rights of the freed slaves. Every fifty years there is a gathering of the many members of the Sturge family to visit the Quaker burial ground at Hazel, not far away, and to visit the old homes of the Sturges, including Elberton Manor. The last gathering was in 1980.

Elberton Manor contains a splendid Jacobean staircase with fine carving and long pendulous, skilfully carved projections under the newels and is very similar to one at Wick Court. A number of the doors are original and some have Tudor rose carvings at the base of the door frames, while on an upper floor is an apostle door with twelve panels. Several windows have been blocked in, probably due to the window tax of the eighteenth century and a number of the windows still retain their hood moulds.

About two miles to the north-west and a mile from the Severn is Littleton upon Severn, once a tiny port supplying the district with coal from the Forest of Dean and South Wales and the local brickworks with sand and clay. It also exported bricks to where they were needed, and dealt with fish from the Severn.

The little church, with its saddle-back roof, is dedicated to St Mary de Malmesbury and was once attached to Malmesbury Abbey. In the late nineteenth century, it was in such a bad state of repair that it had to be demolished to foundation level, including the tower, and rebuilt. However, there are many items from the old church, including the fine Norman font with its chevron design and the two piscinas inserted in the wall by the altar table. Around the foot of the font are tiles from Thornbury Castle. Their devices are heraldic, including the arms of Stafford, Duke of Buckingham. The emblems round it comprise a reef knot, known as the Stafford Knot, the flaming axle box representing Woodstock, the Brecknock Mantle of the Lord of Brecon and the chained swan representing de Bohun of the Lordship of Southampton. The floor of the church is rich in seventeenth- and eighteenth-century ledger stones.

A great event in Littleton upon Severn was the arrival of a whale in 1885 in Littleton Pill. The animal had become stranded on the river bed during the outgoing tide. With ropes and steam traction engines, the locals managed to heave it to the bank, where in two weeks over 40,000 people came to see it, many walking the four miles from Thornbury, where public transport from Bristol ended.

Whale Wharf is still a reminder of the incident and the brickworks which stood on the bank was renamed the Whale Brick, Tile and Pottery Works. Like the whale, the brickworks has gone and the small compact site is now used by several small firms as offices and stores, a kind of miniature trading estate, adjoining the abandoned wharf from which the *Matilda* used to ply. A boat club still finds a use for the old wharf, but as to the *Matilda*, her hull rots in the pill and now there is little to be seen of her above the mud.

Fishing is still an industry at Littleton upon Severn by means of what are known as "fixed engines", although there is nothing mechanical about them at all—just racked frames on which are set rows of putchers, conical basket traps with their mouths towards the incoming tide to catch the salmon on their way up river. Before the Oldbury Nuclear Power Station was erected, Littleton had the largest fixed engine, holding eight hundred and fifty putchers. In recent years, however, salmon fishing has decreased.

Oldbury village, like Littleton, is described as "upon Severn", although again it is a mile or so from the river. These village names would have been more accurate in the past as they were villages of the marshland, subject to severe flooding. During the seventeenth and eighteenth centuries, much of the land was drained by numerous rhines or pills, converting low-lying flood areas into pasture and cider apple orchards. From the rich pasture land came the famous Double Gloucester cheese. It is interesting to note that Brian Waters in his book *Severn Tide* of 1947 mentions that Double Gloucester cheese was hard to come by, but now, like many regional cheeses, it is produced commercially and is to be found in any supermarket. What is hard to come by is the farmhouse cider or "scrumpy" which used to be made round the villages of Severnside, although there are still a few places where it is made and one farmer at Oldbury has decided to revive the local cider making in quite a big way. One of the most potent varieties in this area was made from the Kingston Black apple and if one was not used to scrumpy it could have quite disastrous results.

The area round Oldbury is flat, but interspersed by slightly elevated land and knolls and it is on such knolls that the churches are often built. They, at least, were out of the floods. The one at Oldbury is conspicuous on its isolated hill and it is worth climbing up to the church if only for the view, with the Severn Bridge downstream and upstream the great concrete towers of the Oldbury Nuclear Power Station. Across the estuary can be seen Chepstow, the Forest of Dean and the foothills of the Welsh Mountains.

The church is dedicated to a local saint, Arilda, who was martyred at Kington between Littleton and Thornbury, beheaded by a frustrated suitor. The church was destroyed by fire in 1897 and was rebuilt with the exception of the north porch and the tower. There was a spire until 1703, when it was damaged by a hurricane and had to be removed. There is a legend, not peculiar to Oldbury, that when the church was first built, it was intended to be in the village, but the work was destroyed each night. The villagers consulted an aged hermit, who told them to yoke together two maiden heifers and to build the church where they stopped. The heifers preferred the grazing on the knoll and so the church was built there.

The two public houses at Oldbury are "The Ship" and "The Anchor", testifying to Oldbury's connection with the Severn for like Littleton, Oldbury was a port for coal from the other side of the estuary. The fishing was rich in salmon, flat-fish and shrimps, while there were eels and ducks in the pills. Oldbury is a more compact village than Littleton. Old-world cottages with flowering gardens cluster round the two inns and taper out towards the church on the hill, while Littleton straggles along the green lanes towards the estuary, with a few fine seventeenth-century farmhouses, but both villages have retained their characteristic charm with surprisingly little modern development.

Further north on the bank of the Severn is Sheperdine, with its well-known public house "The Windbound". For many years it was merely a nickname for the New Inn, but it became so familiarly known as "The Windbound" that the name was changed. It owes this name to the bargees who used to ply with their coal vessels up and down the Severn and put in for a drink at the New Inn. On many occasions it was more than one drink and sometimes they were in no state to proceed further. Their excuse to their masters was that they had been "windbound". The building has often been flooded on excessively high tides and strong winds when the river has come over the adjoining sea wall and water has poured down the chimneys.

A little further to the north-east and the last village within Avon on the road to Berkeley is Hill, another village with an elevated church, as its name implies, although it was previously known as Hull. Both church and manor house are perched high up on a slope with two parallel drives leading to them. As at Elberton only the garden wall separates the manor house, Hill Court, from the churchyard. Until 1979 there was no made road up to the church and funeral and wedding groups had to climb the hill by the winding footpath. When the weather was too bad, they sometimes reached the church by way of the Court. Now, due to a generous gift of a parishioner who found the going difficult, the steep track has been tarmacadamed with a parking and turning space for cars at the top. We were told that ours was the first visitor's car to travel on the newly made surface.

The church of St Michael has a fourteenth-century tower with a spire and a thirteenth-century chancel, but the atmosphere is delightfully Georgian, for the nave was rebuilt by the lord of the manor, Sir Francis Fust, in 1759 with its white plastered walls, large light windows and canopied manorial box pew. Although there was restoration and repair in the nineteenth and twentieth centuries, the body of the church is still untouched. The thir-teenth-century chancel with its lancet window has a door on the south side leading to the eighteenth-century, but restored, mortuary chapel of the Jenner-Fust family who occupy Hill Court. The original family was that of the Fusts but at the end of the eighteenth century the male line died out and the property eventually passed to a relative who added his name of Jenner to the old name of Fust. One branch of the Jenner family is con-nected with Dr Jenner, famous for his work on vaccination and who is buried at Berkeley. Within the chapel are various heraldic shields associated with the Jenner-Fusts.

At the west end of the church is a memorial to Sir John Fust who died in 1779. The memorial tells us that "he was of the middle stature of a benign and comely countenance, expressive of his mind which was active amiable and generous". It is not often that we get a description of appearance on a memorial tablet. Buried in the same vault is Dame Phillipa Fust who died in 1805 and the memorial tells us that she "exemplified every Chris-tian virtue" and that "by strenuous exertions she rescued the innocent from the snares of seduction" and "she was chiefly instrumental in securing from a deep scene of villany, the family estate to its lawful successors". This no doubt refers to the difficult time when there were no male heirs.

Hill Court itself was rebuilt in 1863-4 and is much smaller than its predecessor. The village itself is tiny, a scattering of cottages and houses at the foot of the hill.

South-east of Hill is Rockhampton. Although some distance from the Severn, it was subject to flooding and in 1606 flood waters drowned people and cattle. In fact, the whole area around

Hill was described as a miserable region, swampy and malaria ridden, but in 1750 Sir Francis Fust, who rebuilt much of Hill church, had great drainage works carried out and reclaimed much land for pasture and crops. The nucleus of Rockhampton is a *cul-de-sac* with just the church of St James, rebuilt but still with its fourteenth-century tower and ancient door, the old village school and four white modern council houses, all charmingly arranged around the village green.

Falfield is on the A38 trunk road, once the principal road from Bristol to the north before the motorway was constructed. The church of St George at Falfield was built in 1860, but the most conspicuous feature at Falfield is the nineteenth-century mansion Eastwood Park, on the slope to the west of the road. It is now a Detention Centre for juveniles but its first use by the Home Office was in the war years, when it became, with Easingwold in Yorkshire, an anti-gas school for training air-raid wardens. This was extended to fire fighting and rescue work and for this purpose in its grounds was built a "ruined village", even with a crashed plane. It later became a police college for training police in special task work.

The small town of Thornbury lies half-way between Bristol and Gloucester to the west of the A38. Its greatest historical association is with Edward Stafford, Duke of Buckingham, who lost his head during Henry VIII's reign, for here the ill-fated Duke built his castle on the edge of the town.

Years ago, we were shown over the castle by the occupant, Sir Algar Howard, Garter King at Arms and Black Rod, who went before the Queen at the opening of Parliament and knocked at the door of the Commons for permission to enter. The Howards had lived there since the beginning of the eighteenth century, but at the time of my visit, in connection with an Italian prisoner-of-war camp in the grounds, the castle was only partly occupied. The ground floor is now an exclusive restaurant and its light and roomy kitchen is entered from the courtyard arch. The kitchen is floored with tiles similar to those at Littleton upon Severn's church, bearing the Buckingham arms and charges. In fact there are reminders of Buckingham everywhere. A stone carved doorway bears his emblems in relief, the fiery axle of Woodstock, the Brecknock Mantle, the Stafford Knot, among other devices. The Knot even appears on the mounting block in the courtyard. Fireplaces, too, display the emblems. The upper floors of the castle are residential quarters and the grounds actually contain a fair-sized vineyard. The white German-type wine is pressed and prepared in one of the courtyard buildings, within a stone's throw of the restaurant where it will be consumed, although the locally produced wine is only part of the cellar.

Edward Stafford, 3rd Duke of Buckingham and great grandson of Edward III, started to build the castle in 1511, but it was never finished, for Henry VIII, suspicious of his ambitions, which some said reached to the throne itself, summoned him to London on a charge of high treason in 1521 and he was beheaded on Tower Hill. The castle was confiscated by the King, who stayed there with Anne Boleyn for some days in 1533, prevented from visiting Bristol by plague in the city. The chief citizens had to come to Thornbury to visit him. The castle was restored to the Staffords by Queen Mary in 1554 and eventually passed by marriage into the hands of the Howard family, until it was sold in the 1960s. During the seventeenth and eighteenth centuries, the interior of the castle fell into ruins, but was partly restored in the nineteenth century and again in recent times.

Churches are often away from the village and close to the manor house, so it is not surprising that Thornbury church is away from the centre of the town and adjoins the castle. Although a Norman church once stood here, the only traces of Norman work in the present church are the transitional Norman north and south doorways and these are insertions, no doubt salvaged from the older church. The chancel, which is restored, dates from the mid fourteenth century and the south aisle was added a little later with the Stafford chapel displaying the Stafford Knot. On the roof corbels are the arms of the lords of the manor, including William Rufus, Fitzhamon, de Clare, Stafford and Howard. It is said that once a gallery ran from the castle to the north wall of the chancel with a small room and window through which the Duke and his family could see into the church.

Thornbury, itself, a little up the hill, has all the airs of a thriving country town and indeed it is, for it is a market town, enjoying its own form of isolation. It may have traffic problems at times, but these are its own, for the main highway from Bristol to Gloucester, the A38, passes to the east of the town and, long before the existence of the A38, the old turnpike road avoided it as far back as 1769, leaving Thornbury something of a backwater, keeping its old streets and buildings. The main street layout, the letter Y formed by the junction of Castle Street, High Street and the Plane, has not changed since medieval times, for so it is described in the itinerary of Henry VIII's antiquary, Leland.

Across the High Street, two enormous creatures almost face each another, a swan and a lion, crowning what are two fine ornamental porches, of almost identical design, of the eighteenth-century Swan and White Lion Hotels. Along the streets, the buildings range through the centuries with a whole variation of designs, including the well-preserved old Market House and the small Greek temple built in 1839 which was the old Registry office.

The present market is by the railway station, closed in 1967, but until 1911 the market, including a cattle market, was held in the open street. Although once essentially an agricultural town, Thornbury now has other industries in an industrial estate on its south-east fringe. Its population today has increased enormously and many of the residents work in Filton, Bristol and at the Nuclear Power Station at Oldbury. In 1980 a large sports centre was opened, which included facilities for swimming and all kinds of sport. In spite of its ancient buildings, there is nothing static about Thornbury, for it is already planning its amenities for the future and for an increased population, but always with a thought for the conservation of those buildings which are part of the town's tradition.

Around the junction of the Thornbury and Aust roads with the A38, adjoining the Ship Inn, a seventeenth- and eighteenth-century tavern, and the Post House Hotel, we find the village of Alveston, with its Victorian church of 1885. Near the Ship Inn is the cricket pitch on which W. G. Grace and his brother played. The Thornbury Cricket Club which plays on the same pitch was founded in 1872 by the "Coroner", the familiar title given to W. G.'s brother, E. M. Grace, also a celebrated cricketer.

Much of Alveston consists of large housing estates on the west side of the A38, but the old settlement of farmhouses and cottages are centred round the medieval church on the east side, approached by a road from Rudgeway, a hamlet incorporated into Alveston. Of the old church, little is left but the empty shell of the fifteenth-century tower and one nave wall, with an early Norman opening, now blocked. A large solitary yew still stands in the churchyard, although many of the old grave slabs have been cleared to one side and the Norman font is now in the newer church. Here are some fine sixteenth- and seventeenth-century buildings.

Until about 1900, one of Alveston's cottage industries was teasel growing. The dried teasels were sent to woollen factories where the heads were used for roughing up the cloth. Another local industry, like many places in this area, was quarrying. Today, Alveston is so close to Bristol that it has become a dormitory suburb for that town, as its extensive housing estates indicate.

From most places on the A38 from Upper Almondsbury, through Rudgeway and Alveston, the old Roman route from Gloucester to Abonae (Sea Mills), there are marvellous views on a clear day. From this ridgeway, you can look across the Severn Valley, with the shining line of the river and the great towers of the Severn Bridge to the Forest of Dean, the Gwent mountains and often to the higher mountains beyond.

South-west of Alveston and a mile apart are Tockington and Olveston. Tockington still keeps its village green, although its manor house is now a school. The entrance front is eighteenth century, but the building itself dates from the sixteenth century. In the eighteenth century, the manor was held, through marriage, by Sir Jon Dineley Goodere. His brother Samuel, a naval captain, had Sir Jon seized in Bristol and brought aboard his ship, H.M.S. *Ruby*, where he was strangled. It is said that Samuel hoped to get his brother's possessions, but instead he was hanged on the gallows on St Michael's Hill, Bristol. At the three-hundred-year-old pub "The Swan", the beer is kept cool by a natural spring in the cellar. Tockington, as a village, is a charming place, with its old houses surrounding the green.

At Olveston are the fifteenth-century remains of Olveston Court at Olveston Court Farm. Part of the battlemented wall and part of the moat still remain, but the most attractive part is the two-storeyed Tudor gatehouse, with its fine four-centred arch. Other parts, such as doorways and fragments of walling have been incorporated into the farm buildings. The house was once occupied by the Dennis family, who acquired so many of the large houses in the neighbourhood at various times. Brasses of members of the Dennis family are to be seen in the church, which is interesting for its typically late Norman tower, rebuilt in 1604 after severe storm damage and its fourteenth-century features. In the main street close to the nineteenth-century post office is a pleasant row of eighteenth-century cottages. The elegant buildings here, as in other neighbouring villages, no doubt owe their origin to rich Bristol merchants, who as well as their Bristol town houses, wanted houses in the country, but near enough to travel into town on business.

East of the A38 and M5 is Gaunts Earthcott, a small hamlet, worth a visit to see the sixteenth-century manor house, for although a datestone tells us that it was built in 1603, parts of the building are earlier. When Maurice de Gaunt founded Gaunt's Hospital in Bristol in the thirteenth-century, he endowed the establishment with various manors, including Gaunts Earthcott. The house is now a restaurant.

Part of the village of Almondsbury is on the A38 ridgeway, but most of it clusters round the church at the bottom of the hill and from the A38, its church's lead spire can be seen rising from below. Modern housing development began earlier than in Alveston, as the village is nearer Bristol, so that the large compact housing estates are not a feature and it still has very much of a village atmosphere. The Rev B. G. Carne of Almondsbury told me that the village had preserved its identity partly because of its position. On one side the Severn marshes, subject to much flooding in the past, had limited its expansion westward, while the steep scarp on the east had curbed building in that direction and modern development had been limited to small groups around the village.

The church has a Norman north porch and font and its elegant, diagonally patterned lead spire is one of only three in the country, the others being at Godalming, Surrey, and at Swingbridge, Devon. One of the windows in the church was restored in 1931 to the memory of Charles Richardson, the originator and engineer of the Severn Tunnel. On the wall of the church, just west of the north door is a tablet to two children, John and Elizabeth Maronje, who died in 1708 and 1711. Their father, a Frenchman, had the memorial erected in the belief that their death was a retribution for his own sins. According to the former landlord of the "Blue Bowl", the inn was haunted by a six-year-old French girl and two women. He believed that the girl was Elizabeth Maronfe. The publican's daughter is said to have seen the child and heard her reciting rhymes and the publican heard the child talking and crying.

A half mile from Almondsbury, above the Cattybrook Brick Works, a fifteenth-century tower marks the site of Knole Park, the scene of one of the strangest events in Almondsbury's history. In the house in 1817 lived Samuel Worrall, formerly Town Clerk of Bristol, when the peace of his household was disturbed by a young girl. She arrived in the village, wearing what seemed to be eastern clothes. She did not appear to understand English and conveyed by signs that her name was Caraboo. The villagers took her to the overseer, who in turn took her to Squire Worrall and with the help of his library and a Portuguese sailor who pretended to understand her, it was finally decided that she was an eastern princess, captured by pirates and that she had escaped by jumping overboard in the Bristol Channel. Well provided for at Knole Park, her fame spread far and wide and she was entertained at many a fashionable Bath house. Eventually, her fame spread too wide and it came to the attention of her former landlady, a Mrs Neale of Bristol, who recognized her from the newspaper accounts as Mary Baker, the daughter of a Devon cobbler. Money was raised for her to go to Philadelphia, whence she returned after a time and settled in Bristol, where she died in 1865.

South-west of Almondsbury, on the road to Easter Compton, is Over Court, a fine Elizabethan house so damaged by vandalism that it is now a ruin. The archway leading to it is eighteenth century. The house was reputed to have been haunted by a "white lady".

5

The Vale of Sodbury

Filton, astride the A38 road from Bristol to Gloucester, has been so subject to urban development that there are now no signs of a village. In fact, there is nothing to distinguish it from the adjoining part of Bristol and yet it has managed to retain its separate identity. From 1976-9, it even had a mayor, but on a change of council, the title reverted to that of chairman. There is no doubt that it is the most highly industrialized area in Avon outside the cities of Bristol and Bath, for, with adjoining Patchway, it is famous for its aeronautical industry. Who has not heard of the Brabazon, the Britannia and the Concorde? We remember seeing the first Brabazon make its test flight from Filton. The village of Charlton was completely demolished to lengthen the runway. Today, the enormous Brabazon assembly hall, seen from the A38, is a lone witness of the undertaking.

Before 1910, farming or work in Bristol were the only occupations open to residents of Filton. In 1910, the aeroplane company was founded at Filton House, the old bus depot made into a factory and a two-acre meadow into a flying field. Today, the premises of British Aerospace occupy over a third of the parish of Filton and, apart from extensive playing fields, the whole of the remainder is developed. The Parish Council is one of the few in the country to build and administer their indoor swimming-pool and initiated twinning relationships with both French and German communities. The parish church of St Peter has an ancient tower, surmounted by a modern steeple, but because of restoration and rebuilding has lost most of its medieval character. There are some old tombstones to the west of the church. Three side by side are to the two teenage daughters and baby son of William and Elizabeth Millett who lost their three children within a few days of each other in 1745.

Adjoining Filton is Patchway, which is supposed to have derived its name from an ancient trackway. It has been considerably developed for housing, particularly since the last war. It is the home of Rolls Royce Aero Division and many of the residents work in the aeronautical industry or in the light industrial undertakings which have grown up on its border. The New Inn at Patchway was once a coaching station and the old stables are now a dining-room.

Not far from Filton and Patchway is Stoke Gifford, which derives its name from a member of the Giffard family, who held it, with other manors, from the Conqueror, until it was confiscated by King John because one of the family took part in a rebellion against him. The manor was restored and then lost again and eventually it was transferred to John Maltravers as a reward for his part in the murder of Edward II at Berkeley Castle. Eventually the land passed to the Berkeley family and then to the Beauforts by the marriage of Elizabeth, sister and heir of Norborne Berkeley, Lord Botetourt, who was Governor of Virginia in the eighteenth century and who died there.

Those who use the Parkway Railway Station on the main line to London and South Wales may notice, behind the mass of cars in the car park, the old grey stone church of St Michael and if they leave the station and go round the corner, they may be surprised to find a charming rural scene: a green complete with chestnut trees, the fourteenth-century church in one corner, some Victorian houses and school, and the "Beaufort Arms" across the road. One of the outstanding features of the church is its north porch with the decorated ogee arched entrance, but the church was much restored in the eighteenth century and the white plastered interior is light and airy, with monuments to the Berkeley family. The vestry, once open to the chancel, was known as the Duchess of Beaufort's room and was provided with a fireplace and furniture where the family could enjoy the service in comfort.

The title of the Duchess of Beaufort lives on for the manor house of the Berkeleys and later the Dower House of the Beauforts, Stoke Park, is still generally known as the "Duchess's". A manor house was built in the sixteenth century and rebuilt by Lord Botetourt about 1760. It stands high on a huge artificial mound, overlooking its park. The park contained what

Thornbury Castle

Village green, Tockington

Lower Almondsbury

Village shop, Frenchay

Hambrook from Whiteshill Common

Churchyard cross, Iron Acton

The Tortworth Chestnut

Railway station, Charfield

Modern shopping centre, Yate

Upton House, Upton Cheyney

Swainswick

The Marshfield Mummers

St Peter's Church adjoining Dyrham House

Duckpond, Hawkesbury Upton

Toll house, Acton Turville

Village Hall, Priston

were thought to be prehistoric burial mounds, but we excavated one of them some years ago and decided it was a "folly". Stoke Park or the "Duchess's" is now a hospital.

Because of its proximity to Filton and Bristol, housing development has increased considerably in modern times, particularly in part of the parish known as Little Stoke where there are large housing estates. We were told that there is still felt to be a barrier between residents of the old village and the new-comers.

Frenchay, with its old houses strung round the edge of Frenchay Common, still has every appearance of a village. The church on the Common was built in only 1834, but Frenchay's religious history goes back much further for, like much of the Kingswood district, it was a fervent nonconformist area. The Friends' Meeting House, opposite the present-century village hall, was first erected in 1673 and rebuilt in 1809. Not only did the local Quakers attend there, but also people like Joseph Storr Fry from Bristol, whose humble business eventually culminated in the large chocolate factory at Somerdale, Keynsham. No doubt Frenchay was a reasonably quiet place in which to gather outside the city, but even there in 1677, John Meredith, J.P., attacked the congregation and damaged the meeting house. Many of the attractive houses round Frenchay Common were built by Quakers who settled there. The Manor House was built in 1736, probably designed by John Wood the Elder for Joseph Beck, a Quaker linen merchant. Thomas Callowhill lived at Frenchay Lodge and his daughter became the second wife of William Penn, whose name is perpetuated in Pennsylvania. Pennsylvania was actually mortgaged in 1708 by Penn in respect of a loan from Callowhill of £6800. Cedar Hall, south of the Friends' Meeting House, was lived in by Edward Harford, who was a Quaker banker. A Quaker school was held there in the mid nineteenth century.

In 1689, the Toleration Act was passed which granted free right of worship to all Protestant nonconformists. In 1720, the Unitarians built their chapel opposite the common and at Clarendon House, they set up a school in the nineteenth century. Now Clarendon House and Frenchay House have become luxury hotels for retired people, and the Manor a children's home, examples of the changing use of old houses.

The oldest part of Frenchay is at the far side of the Common by the tiny bridge over the River Frome, In fact, Frenchay derives its name from the river and was formerly known as Fromeshaw,

"shaw" being a spinney. The Frome here, as elsewhere, provided driving power for mills and Frenchay once had a factory making farm implements, sold not only in this country, but also abroad. In 1979, a woman in the village told me that several of the old cottages had been demolished and modern houses erected on their sites, while others had been sold to newcomers for considerable sums and totally renovated, but on the whole the district around the Common is unspoilt and since it was made a conservation area in 1975, it is fortunately preserved against any undesirable development. Of the various games played on the Common, none was so spectacular as the cricket played by the Graces in the mid nineteenth century, especially when one of the family hit the church clock.

North of Frenchay is Hambrook which at the time of the Domesday Book was a separate manor, but later joined to that of Winterbourne. It once had a wool factory, when wool was the principal industry of the area. An old mill was still used for corn grinding at the beginning of this century, but its ruins disappeared when the motorway was constructed. There are still quite a few old houses in the area, but the character of the village has changed bacause of modern development. There is now an attractive walk along the banks of the Frome which links Hambrook with other villages.

The present White Horse Inn was built about 1800, but the previous building is believed to be that mentioned by Fielding in 1749 in *Tom Jones* as "a very creditable house". By the inn is Hambrook Grove of eighteenth-century origin. Hambrook House is earlier being seventeenth century, but it was altered about 1784. The eighteenth-century Hambrook Court was once tenanted by Lieutenant-Colonel, Thomas Brereton, who commanded the troops during the Bristol Riots of 1831 and who committed suicide because of the general condemnation over his lack of strong action against the rioters.

Whiteshill, north of the M4 motorway, is part of Winterbourne and no longer distinguishable from it. Indeed the proximity to Bristol of this whole area has meant the destruction of much of its rural character.

Winterbourne has changed over the years from an agricultural village to very much a dormitory area for Bristol workers and yet its oldest part has remained untouched. This is the area round Winterbourne church, quite some distance from the main road where much of the development has taken place. In this quiet oasis, the buildings are a few cottages, the church and the adjoining Winterbourne Court Farm and its dovecot. It has been suggested that this may have been the nucleus of the village until the mid seventeenth century, when, because of the pennant grit quarrying, the road was diverted to its present route where the new village grew up. However, there is no evidence that the settlement round the church was any larger than today.

As well as its quarries, Winterbourne had its beaver hat industry, which flourished for a hundred years from 1770 to 1870, when the broad-rimmed beaver hat gave way to the cheaper and lighter silk hat from France, resulting in the failure of an industry which had provided work for several hundred people in Winterbourne and the surrounding area. At Watleys End, between Winterbourne and Frampton Cotterell, one hat factory employed over one hundred men and when this industry declined, many residents, particularly women, had to seek employment in Bristol clothing factories. Hat making was also a cottage industry and the trade's failure meant hardship for many cottagers.

Winterbourne church is dedicated to St Michael, but like that of Stoke Gifford, it lacks the mount upon which churches of St Michael usually stand. Part of its chancel is of late twelfth century and a number of other features belong to the fourteenth century. There is a romantic story about an effigy of a knight by the north wall of the church. He is reputed to have been Hugo de Sturden, the Hickory Stern immortalized by Robert Lucas Pearsall in his song, "Oh, Who will o'er the Down so free?" He eloped with the Dennis lady who had been locked in her room at Syston Court and rode with her over Winterbourne Down. Although the hero of the adventure at Syston, de Sturden seems to have been something of a rogue and was outlawed for certain unsavoury deeds. Tradition says that he made a pact with the devil. In return for certain favours, he agreed that when he died, he would neither be carried into the church head or feet forward nor be buried in the churchyard, but he cheated even the devil for he instructed his coffin to be carried in sideways, and deposited in the wall. The effigy, however, is not in its original position and there are doubts about whether it really is of Hugo de Sturden. The church contains some memorials to the Bradestone family, who originally held the manor, and on the wall is a brass of about 1370 of one of the Bradestone ladies wearing a veiled head-dress. Her dress has pocket holes showing part of the girdle beneath and is believed to be the oldest brass in the county.

The old manor house of the Bradestones, where Ebenezer Ludlow, the Bristol town clerk, lived during the Bristol riots of 1831, was burned down in 1881 and has been replaced by Winterbourne Court Farm. The dovecot, of which you can see the roof from the churchyard, is all that remains of the old buildings. The relationship between the Bradestones and the church was not always good and Anthony Bradestone during the sixteenth century was accused of taking possession of lands and tenements belonging to the chantry of St Michael. He later appointed his own priest, Rastall, for the chantry, but another claimed the patronage of the chantry and presented his own candidate. In 1541 the matter was referred to the Vicar General who found Rastall unqualified, unsuitable and a gambler.

The name of Winterbourne means an intermittent stream which flows in winter, but dries up in summer, the "bourne" being the Bradley Brook.

The name of Coalpit Heath to the east of Winterbourne describes the village just as clearly, for coal-mining activities there gave employment to many people in the area, The industry did not close down until 1949 when the last pit at Frog Lane was forced to close because of flooding from an abandoned pit at Parkfield. The closure of Frog Lane meant the complete cessation of coal mining north of the River Avon, except for work at Harry Stoke which began in 1955 as the result of a sudden urge by the Government to open surface seams by open-cast methods. However, the Harry Stoke project lasted only eight years and today all that remains is the enormous grass-covered mount which is seen on the right of Filton Lane between Filton and Frenchay.

As its name implies Coalpit Heath was one of those heathland areas which existed within and around the edge of the old Royal Forest. Much of them became common land, hence the numerous commons in the district. It was on such land that coal mining first began. One of the difficulties at Coalpit Heath was distribution and so the nine-mile stretch of the Bristol and Gloucestershire Railway was opened in 1835 to connect the Orchard Colliery at Coalpit Heath with the Floating Basin in Bristol. It is an interesting point that our present-day anxiety about the life of oil supplies had its counterpart in 1871 when a Royal Commission reported that if the then present rate of coal consumption increased "even in an approximate degree" our coal supply would be rapidly exhausted.

It was at Coalpit Heath in 1844-5 that the famous architect

William Butterfield built his first church and vicarage. Butterfield built them in Gothic style, according to the trend of the time. It is a beautifully proportioned church and regarded as one of outstanding architectural interest, but the originality of Butterfield's massive lych-gate often attracts more attention than the church. The vicarage, too, built by Butterfield in 1845, is a fine example of the adaptation of the Gothic style to secular buildings. A former vicar told me that living at the vicarage was one of the most pleasant periods of his life, except when the heating bills arrived.

Between Winterbourne and Iron Acton is Frampton Cotterell, once famous, like Winterbourne, for hat making. It had iron mines which closed about 1875 and, like the old California coal pit at Oldland, are now used as a water reservoir. Evidence of iron mine workings can still be seen in a wood on the outskirts of the village. The deep-hewn scars are similar to those in the "scowles" of the Forest of Dean. The entrances have been partly filled in, but the top of one large vertical shaft appears as a rather greenish woodland pool and close by large stone slabs cover yet another shaft. These mines were once a source of employment for the people of the area.

At Frampton Cotterell, the London firm of Christy's, who found labour cheaper there than in the City, established a felt hat making factory in 1818. The old factory buildings still stand at the entrance to the fairground operators' winter storage site. The small closely spaced windows indicate the tiny rooms in which the hat makers had to work. Even these windows had to be kept shut so that the rabbit fur which was added to the wool would not blow away. Mercury was used in the processes and in these close working conditions was said to have affected the brains of some hatters, hence the saying "as mad as a hatter". When the factory closed in 1871 because of a decline in the trade, the firm offered its employees work in London or Stockport. The Frampton Cotterell factory was a late-comer as felt hats had been made in Avon since the sixteenth century, usually as a cottage industry. While the fashionable beaver hat was a felt hat with an outer skin of beaver fur, the felt hat was a shaped and stiffened woollen and rabbit fur hat. Not only did the rich merchants of Bristol benefit from the sugar plantations of the West Indies through their slave and sugar traffic, but so did the cottagers, for felt hats were necessary to protect their wearers against the sun on the plantations.

Although the church of St Peter was rebuilt with the exception of the fifteenth-century tower in 1858, it has retained some of its older monuments and treasures, such as the brass to John Symes of 1661 and the chained copy of Bishop Jewel's *Apology for the Church of England* dated 1568.

North of Frampton Cotterell, we leave development behind and come to the rural village of Iron Acton. Like Winterbourne and Coalpit Heath, the origin of its name is obvious for iron was once worked here. Iron Acton may be described as an example of ancient ribbon development, for most of its buildings are in the road leading down from the main road to the church, a road full of interesting and ancient houses.

The church is built on ground raised above the road and a notable feature is the elaborate early fifteenth-century church-yard cross, a memorial to one of the Poyntz family, who once held sway in Iron Acton and district. Within the church are more reminders of this family. High up in the corner of the Poyntz chapel is a helmet, a spur and leather from a surcoat reputed to have been carried on the coffin of Sir John Poyntz, who died in 1680 and who was the last of the family to be lord of the manor. On the floor in front of the altar are ledger stones of Robert Poyntz (1359-1439), with his wives Anne and Catherine on either side. That of Catherine is barely legible, having been masked by an inscription of 1631 to Elizabeth Poyntz. The Poyntzes were related to the Tudors and entertained Elizabeth I and Sir Francis Drake in their mansion of Acton Court on the road to Latteridge. The sixteenth-century house was new then and Sir Walter Raleigh is said to have frightened the ladies when lighting the newly introduced tobacco in his pipe while walking in the gardens. It is a pity that this grand old house with skewed chimneys is falling into decay.

There were once two manors in the neighbourhood, that of Iron Acton with its manor house, Acton Court and Ilgar, later part of Iron Acton, with the house known as Algars Manor, by a pleasant little bridge over the Frome. Although originally Tudor, the present house is mainly eighteenth century. Along the bank of the Frome, hardly big enough here to be called a river, the present owner of Algars Manor has allowed part of his land to be used as a public river walk and nature trail and a pleasant walk it is too.

An interesting building in Iron Acton is the Lamb Inn with its "1690" bar, and almost opposite is a cottage called "The Nook", of similar design and gabled like the inn, bearing the date 1688.

Some iron working on a small scale was once carried out at Iron Acton and some of the scars can still be seen.

North of Iron Acton, on the B4058 road, is Rangeworthy, a village easily missed as it straggles along the road with no defined centre. The village and its surroundings appear rather nondescript, for its two attractive features, the church and the Court, are away off the road. Holy Trinity Church was partly rebuilt in the fifteenth and sixteenth centuries and restored in 1857, but still contains some Norman features. Rangeworthy Court is a fine gabled manor house with mullioned and hood moulded windows. Sir Matthew Hale, Lord Chief Justice of England to Charles II, lived there and added the tall gabled porch in 1664. The Lord of the Manor, Hugh de Audley, is said to have stayed in this house, or its predecessor, with his wife Margaret in the fourteenth century. She had unfortunate family connections, for her previous husband Piers Gaveston had been beheaded as was her father the Earl of Gloucester and she was the niece of Edward II, murdered at Berkeley.

Near the M5 motorway, we find Tytherington, a village where limestone quarrying has developed to a large scale. The church of St James is thirteenth and fifteenth century, with extensive late nineteenth-century restoration. It has a curious one-handed clock and its mechanism is said to date back to the early sixteenth century. Inside the church, on the wall near the font, is a small, rectangular brass plaque, engraved with an hour glass, wings, shovel, skull and cross bones and is a memorial to Richard Bromwick, who died in 1753.

Diagonally opposite the church is the Swan Inn, which appropriately enough is in Duck Lane, for here was once the village pond, complete we may assume with ducks and possibly a swan or two. Some idea of the age of the inn may be gained by a record of Isaac Stick, who was the landlord in 1608. It has a fine ancient exterior, but although the bar has been modernized, it still retains a genuine log fire, rare in these days of gas pseudo-log fires seen in so many public houses. We are told that there was a ghost, something which shuffled across one of the bedrooms. Tytherington has several seventeenth- and eighteenth-century buildings, one of the finest being the seventeenth-century Grange near the church, with its four imposing gables and a nineteenth-century porch.

North-east of Tytherington is Cromhall which is another of those settlements which originally had two manors, Lygon containing most of the village and Cromhall Abbots, now Abbotside, which was given to St Augustine's Abbey, Bristol, in 1148. Lygon was the name of the family who acquired the remaining manor in 1466. The fourteenth- to fifteenth-century church of St Andrew was much restored in 1851. The medieval pulpit is shaped like a chalice on a slender support and is remarkable in that it is entered from the vestry. Cromhall is a very scattered village with several centres along the B4058. At Heath End, a lot of houses border the road, but when you pass these and turn left along Church Lane, you find a typical village nucleus, with the church, school and farmhouses. Next door to the church is Court Farm, but the manor house apparently once stood behind the church on what is now a kitchen garden attached to the farm.

Less than three miles north of Cromhall is Tortworth, which has all the appearance of a private estate, as indeed it was, for some 400 acres of the area forms Tortworth Park. The Court, built about 1850 for the Earls of Ducie, is now a prison officers' training school, while part of its once vast estate is Leyhill open prison. What there is of the village is centred by the village church and its large green. On either side of the road approaching the village are two castellated lodges to the former manor house which adjoined the church. In a field close to the church and surrounded by a fence is the famous Tortworth Chestnut. The seventeenth-century diarist John Evelyn referred to it as the "great chestnut" of King Stephen's time (1135-1154), but it is certainly believed to have been there in King John's reign about 1200. On the gate to the enclosure is the following inscription on a bronze plaque:

This tree supposed to be
Six Hundred Years Old 1st Jany 1800
May Man Still Guard thy Venerable form
From the Rude Blasts and Tempestuous Storms
Still mayest thou Flourish through succeeding time
And Last Long Last the Wonder of the Clime

The tree, a Spanish Chestnut, is gnarled and its great lower limbs rest on the ground, but it still flourishes well. In autumn the ground beneath it is covered with a thick carpet of brown fallen leaves and in early spring with masses of snowdrops.

St Leonard's Church was rebuilt in 1872, but retains its fifteenth-century tower and some fourteenth-century work. The font is Norman and the building contains some fifteenth-century stained glass and two fine canopied tombs of the Throckmorton family. One is that of Thomas Throckmorton who died in 1568 and the other of another Thomas Throckmorton who died in 1607.

North-east of Tortworth is Charfield. Its old church is at Churchend some way south of the main village. The old church is now but a shell, but its churchyard contains in one corner a common grave of the victims of a rail disaster which occurred by the road bridge in Charfield in 1928 when fourteen people were killed. It happened in thick fog at about 5 o'clock in the morning. A goods train was leaving the main line for a siding to clear the line for the Newcastle, Leeds to Bristol express, but had not completely cleared it when the express hit it. Visibility at the time was down to thirty yards. To make matters worse a goods train coming up from Bristol on the other track collided with the wreckage. Carriages were piled up, under and against the bridge. Two bodies were thrown over the bridge, but other victims were trapped in the wreckage which immediately caught fire because of the explosion of gas cylinders used for carriage lighting. The bodies were charred beyond recognition, but two identified as children have always remained a mystery as no relative ever came forward to claim them. In connection with a B.B.C. book review, Mr Oliver Williams, a resident of nearby Wotton under Edge, suggested that they may have been jockeys, as according to him, there were three jockeys on the train, but only one identified. Even then, it was strange that no one enquired about them and so the mystery remains.

Not far from the bridge and close to the Railway Inn, there is an area of ground where can be seen old double- and single-deck buses waiting renovation by a firm which sends them abroad for service. Other industries, such as engineering, are located in old water mills on the Little Avon, while another mill on the same river between Charfield and Tortworth has been converted into the Huntingford Mill Hotel amid attractive river scenery.

It is difficult to imagine that Wickwar, known as Wichen or Wic in the distant past, meaning a farm settlement, was once a prosperous clothing town and that it possessed a mayor and corporation from Edward II's time until the late nineteenth century. It could also boast of electric street lighting before Bristol and probably before most of the rest of the county. In 1890, carbon arc lights were installed in the brewery by a chemist named Ansell who was interested in electricity. When the Wickwar Parish Council was set up under the Local Government Act of 1894, it lost no time in arranging an extension for electric street lighting. Of its two nineteenth-century breweries, one was converted into a cider factory now used for storage. This building can be seen from the churchyard as you look over the valley to the Cotswold escarpment, with the Nibley Monument in the trees on the horizon and the Somerset Monument to the right. Down below, heaps of rubble mark the site of the old railway station. Other industries include British Nylon Spinners and the manufacture of sliding doors.

The inn, once called the New Inn, is now named the Buthay, pronounced "Buttey", and its sign is of an archer. Archery was once practised on the Buthay, an open space, now surrounded by buildings lying just off the main road within the village. The Warre family lived at Wickwar and it is from that family that the town received the second half of its name. In 1627, a fourteen-year-old apprentice, Alexander Hosea, was sent by his master to get a dish of whitepot, a fair day delicacy, from the baker. Unfortunately, but fortunately for Wickwar, he dropped the dish and, scared of the consequences, he fled to London. Unlike Dick Whittington of Gloucestershire, he did not become Lord Mayor, but he did make a fortune and returned to his native town, setting up there in 1684 a school for poor children with provision in his will for a house for the schoolmaster. These buildings still stand in the main street, now as two dwelling-houses.

Another striking building in the wide main street is the Town Hall built at the end of the eighteenth century, with a bellcote and arches. The Town Hall clock is an exceptional one, as the mechanism is thought to date from 1660 and is the only one in the world with an escapement of ninety teeth. It was later converted to the Town Hall clock. Nearby are several houses and buildings of the seventeenth and eighteenth century. Except for the Perpendicular west tower, the church was rebuilt in 1881, but still has some fifteenth- seventeenth- and eighteenth-century treasures, including a fine eighteenth-century "Bristol" type chandelier and a late fifteenth-century sculpture of St John the Baptist which came from the old Tudor manor house, Pool House, which once stood in the terraced garden with a lake south-west of the church. There is a railway tunnel beneath the site of the drained lake and the tower is the air vent.

Sodbury was one of the old Saxon manors and the town of Chipping Sodbury, some four miles south of Wickwar, was set up in the twelfth century by William le Gros, Lord of the Manor.

In 1218, Henry III granted William's grandson a charter for a market and fairs and the grid system street plan was laid out, little changed even today, with the wide market street and the long burgage plots behind its houses, an early example of town planning. "Chipping" means a market and the rest of the manor to the east became known as Old Sodbury to distinguish it from the new town. Its most famous fair was the Mop Fair held twice a year, where labourers and servants would present themselves with some article of their calling, perhaps a mop, to be engaged for a year's work by the local farmers. In later years the Mop Fair became a fun fair, with stalls, roundabouts and the usual fairground apparatus.

The wide street is full of fine sixteenth- to eighteenth-century buildings. Towards the Yate end we have the fine old sixteenth-century Grapes Hotel, with three principal gables and at the other end of the street, near the market area, is a remarkable concentration of inns. In Broad Street is the George Hotel, a late sixteenth- or seventeenth-century building, with steep gables, coach entrance and Georgian windows. On the opposite side of the road are two more inns, "the Royal Oak" and the "Beaufort Hunt", and in Horse Street, facing the entrance of Broad Street, is still another, the "Portcullis", a seventeenth-century coaching inn, where the Beaufort Hunt meets. A small portcullis is one of the charges on the Beaufort Arms. In the eighteenth century, a customer at the inn was a Welshman who bought a local farm, but the amount he spent in the inn was far in excess of a farmer's income. When the authorities found out that the farm merely augmented his principal occupation, that of a highwayman, he was hanged. Many inns have their ghosts. In fact, ghosts seem to prefer inns to houses. The "Portcullis" ghost spends its time outside as a cat wandering the pavement. The story is that an alchemist who discovered the secret of everlasting life, carelessly left the mixture in a saucer and the cat drank it and so prowls for eternity around the inn.

Half way along High Street and standing apart from the line of buildings is the clock tower, now combined with toilets and bus shelter. The wide paving on which they stand used to be the market pitching and further along also on the pitching stands a horse trough and water pump of 1897 set up, it seems to us a little ungraciously, to commemorate Queen Victoria's Diamond Jubilee. Another reminder of the horse transport days are the number of arches in High Street giving access for horse carriages.

In High Street also is the old Grammar School, now the library, but perhaps the most outstanding building is the fifteenth-century Tudor Hall in Hatter's Lane, a name indicative of one of the town's earlier industries. This is an interesting example of a fifteenth-century house and was finally restored in 1957. What has been saved of the old Market Cross has been incorporated into the 1914-18 War Memorial standing at the junction of Broad Street and Horse Street. The church of St John the Baptist was extensively restored in 1869, although of thirteenth-century origin.

Chipping Sodbury flourished as a cloth centre over a long period of time until the trade steadily declined during the eighteenth century. However, situated in an agricultural area, rich in dairy produce, it continued as a thriving market centre. It is still a pleasant place to live and its population has more than trebled since the 1920s. Much of the heavy traffic through the town are stone transporters from the quarries between Chipping Sodbury and Wickwar and the residents complain from time to time about traffic congestion and danger from the lorries. There is a good deal of car traffic as well and parking is often difficult.

Associated with Chipping Sodbury is Yate, the industrial area of the district. Under the Council's Adopted Plan, Chipping Sodbury is retained as a conservation area in contrast to its ever-developing area Yate. With Yate's industrial and housing development, however, have come some pleasant features, such as the Southwold Sports Centre opened in 1974 and its central shopping and pedestrian precinct built in 1965, where its excellent little library, medical centre and shops are centred round an agreeable square. Over the centre of one side of the square is an eye-catching modern spire and the paving slabs carry a piece of modern sculpture, flattish flower bowls and a few round advertising kiosks reminiscent of those in Paris.

In spite of its modern development and high industrial content, Yate is an ancient place. Its very name tells us that, for it is supposed to be derived from Old English *Gete* or *Giet*, a gap or gateway, and it had three manors, centred at Yate Court, Stanshawes and Brinsham. Old Yate is to be found round St Mary's Church. There are Norman remains, but perhaps the most interesting item is the brass of Alexander Staples of Yate Court, who died in 1590, with his two wives Anis and Elizabeth and his eleven children. The two wives are identified by name and his first wife Anis is on his left with her five children and

Elizabeth is on his right with her six children. All the children look alike, but the girls are distinguished by their head-dresses. Yate Court was destroyed by Cromwellian troops, who used it as a garrison headquarters, to prevent it falling into the hands of the Royalists. Eventually its ruins were incorporated into a farm. The only complete building that remained was the fourteenth-century gatehouse and this was removed to Berkeley Castle in Gloucestershire and rebuilt there by the Countess of Berkeley.

The church has a warm, welcoming atmosphere about it and is very much alive to the needs of the modern community. When we last visited it a bazaar was in progress and notices of coffee mornings and other events were much in evidence. Social events were helped by the addition of a new kitchen, the gift of a parishioner in memory of a son who had been killed in an accident, a splendid memorial and a fine contribution to the life of the church congregation. There are far more such amenities in our churches nowadays, echoes of the days when the church ales instead of coffee, were brewed, in the church houses on feast days, but heating is expensive and some churches are still cold and inhospitable, giving the impression that they are more concerned with the dead than with the living.

By the church is St Mary's Church School, built in 1855, now used as a youth centre, and across the small green is the imposing public house and restaurant called Lawns Inn. The façade has been preserved, but although the interior looks ancient, its fine strap plaster type ceiling is merely a good representation of an old ceiling. The landlord told us that when he came there twenty years ago, Yate was a real country village, but the overspill development had altered its character, not for the best for rural life, but good for his business.

Like Chipping Sodbury, Yate was a woollen town and famous for dairy produce. In fact there was a heavy penalty for ploughing up good pasture land.

Yate is famous for celestine or celestite (chemically, strontium sulphate). So rare is it that the material must be recovered by the usual open-cast method before land is developed for building. Some years ago, we remember seeing nodules of this material stacked by roadsides, but there is not much of it today. Its name is derived from "celestial" or "sky blue", although it is usually colourless. It is used for ceramics, fertilizers and refining zinc and beet sugar. Because it burns with a bright red flame it is useful for fireworks, distress and signal flares, tracer shells and, now, colour television. The Yate and Wickwar areas are the only places in Britain, and among the very few places in the world, where it is found. In 1939, Yate produced 95 per cent of the world's supply and in 1979, a plea was made by the Bristol Mineral Company for more land to be put at their disposal.

Yate was one of those areas chosen for post-war Bristol and Bath overspill development and with the enormous increase in housing came increase in industry, although, according to some views, not enough to provide employment for the area and many people in Yate work elsewhere. Although development has joined Chipping Sodbury and Yate, the far greater proportion of industrial and housing estates in Yate, has meant some social division between the two towns.

A little south of Yate is Westerleigh. It was once the western part of the Hundred of Pucklechurch and hence its name. It is said that Westerleigh was given to the monks of Glastonbury on condition that they prayed for the soul of King Edmund, who was murdered at Pucklechurch. Next to the largely fifteenth-century church is a fine row of seventeenth-century cottages, including The Old Inn, which really lives up to its name, a rare find in these days. Although there is a spacious room, we liked the small low-ceilinged bar, one of those into which you might squeeze a dozen if you can open the door to let in the last man. We liked the friendly locals too, although at lunchtime, it is a favourite with workers from Yate.

Not far east of Westerleigh is Wapley, a rural hamlet rather than a village and yet it has a fine church perched on the hillside, overlooking the few houses which make up Wapley. Although restored in 1897, the church contains quite a lot of fourteenth- and fifteenth-century work, including a fifteenth-century box tomb of John Codrington, who died in 1475, at the reputed age of 111 years. He had been appointed standard bearer to Henry V for valour at Agincourt. Below the church is Church Farm, with double-storey porch dated 1636.

Like Wapley, Abson, although almost too small for a village, possesses a fine church. Once held by the abbots of Glastonbury, its name was Abbotston, which was contracted to Abston and finally to Abson. Grouped round a green are most of Abson's cottages, a couple of farms and the church. Inserted into the outside face of the east wall of the chancel is a horizontal phallic human figure, of Saxon or early Norman origin. In the church, dedicated to St James, is an early seventeenth-century pulpit with sounding board. The panels of the box pews removed during restoration in 1901 have been formed into a dado for the church walls, an excellent way of using the eighteenth-century woodwork, and resting against the dado is part of the painted medieval wooden chancel screen.

Although mainly an agricultural village, Abson has a small printing industry, the Abson Press, but it occupies only one house adjoining the green and does not detract from the village green atmosphere.

Just south of Abson is Wick. The new development is chiefly to the north of the main road which is the old Bristol to London turnpike road and was still the usual route from Bristol to London before the M4 motorway was built. The church, adjoining this road, was built in 1845 and, like that at Coalpit Heath, has connections with William Butterfield, the architect, whose work is most conspicuous in the tower and lych-gate. The old village is mainly to the south, and down the lane, nearly opposite the church, is a nineteenth-century mill building, now used for the manufacture of animal feeding stuffs. From the little bridge over the River Boyd can be seen a pretty cascade, not a natural one, but part of the old mill system.

Further up the lane, a side track on the left takes you to Wick Court, built about 1615-20. It is a fine house, cream-stuccoed and gabled. The rear garden side was originally the entrance front and the small gabled room, supported on columns, was added in the early eighteenth century. Inside is a fine Jacobean staircase, not unlike that at Elberton Manor, with its long pendant carvings under the newels. The panelling in the entrance hall is seventeenth century. In one of the first-floor rooms in the dado panelling is a reputed priest hole, so well concealed that, unless you know the correct panel, it can only be found by sounding the woodwork. Inside there is sufficient room to stand and, according to the occupants, it is believed that it once contained an internal staircase leading to the lower floor.

When we first knew the house it was occupied by the Student Christian Movement, but previously it had been occupied by Messrs Partridge and Love, printers, who have the factory on the other side of the river. Early in 1980, it was purchased for use as a private residence again, by two related families, each complete with three generations, forming an extended family group, but a group with an aim, to share their enjoyment of the surroundings with groups of young people. Adjoining the house is a modern building, the Wick Court Centre, managed by the Wycke Foundation, a non profit-making educational trust, providing facilities for students and school children. The centre has dormitory accommodation and bedrooms for fifty people, with a lounge, dining, conference and games rooms. It is a favourite with school project courses in an area rich in natural history and yet within a few miles of Bristol and Bath. The lovely surroundings of the old manor house give a unique experience to many town children.

At the Crown Inn, now the Rose and Crown, at Wick in 1783, was born the boxer John Gully, who did much of his prizefighting at Mangotsfield. He became heavyweight champion in 1808 and was later an M.P. and owned racehorses, winning the Derby on three occasions.

Just above Wick is Doynton, at the foot of the Cotswold edge and by the River Boyd. The village has a number of seventeenth-century gabled houses, including Doynton House. The church is mostly a restoration of the 1860s, but contains some Norman work, a fourteenth-century doorway and a fifteenth-century tower, which is unusually sited on the south side of the chancel. Most of the eighteenth-century buildings in the village show some affinities with the architecture of eighteenth-century Bath, while the old school and playground have been converted into a charming house, a good example of the changing use of village buildings.

6

The Cotswold Fringe

To the east of the county and north of Bath lies the Cotswold scarp and on its top and along its base are strung a number of villages, while some, like North Stoke and Upton Cheyney, are found in the folds of its slopes. North Stoke is approached by a steep lane from the A431 road between Swineford and Kelston. It is hardly more than a hamlet, but its old buildings, like the double-gabled manor farmhouse with the little church of St Martin up on the slope of the hill, make a picturesque setting.

Another uphill climb from the Bath Road brings us to Upton Cheyney, with its attractive old inn, The Upton Inn. We remember it when it was a simple village pub. The landlady was beaten up by intruders and sold it to the present owner, who modernized and enlarged it and the well-furnished bars and restaurant attract a different type of customer. Above the inn and opposite the horticultural glass houses, is Upton House, conspicuous for its bellcote. Here lived the Reverend Parker, who used to summon his men to work by ringing the bell.

East of Upton Cheyney is Langridge in its own combe running down from Lansdown. The lanes running up or down to Langridge are narrow and twisting and, crouched on the remote hillside, is the little church, with its squat Norman tower with its added saddleback roof. There is very little in Langridge other than the church and the late seventeenth-century and part-medieval house adjoining, but the setting is lovely and the church unique. The fourteenth-century porch leads to a Norman doorway, but this is only a foretaste of the treasures which lie beyond. In a niche above the splendid Norman chancel arch is a rough carving of the Madonna and Child, thought to be an unusual example of thirteenth-century work and, through the arch, the chancel and apse end, although restored, give a fine effect of Norman style. The font is thirteenth century and on the floor of the tower is a stone effigy, rather worn, of a lady of the early fourteenth century. A fifteenth-century brass, representing Elizabeth Walsche, in widow's robes, wife of a former lord of the manor, is on the south wall of the nave. A lap dog, with bells on its collar, crouches on the hem of her gown.

The road from Langridge leads up the hill to the top of Lansdown, famous for the civil war battle, where the Royalist leader Sir Bevil Grenville was mortally wounded in 1643. It is said that he was carried to the rectory at Cold Ashton, which is usually accepted, although we have been told that he may have been taken to the building called The Folly. In 1720, a monument was erected on Lansdown, on the site where it is believed he fell.

From Langridge, the road to Bath leads through the little village of Swainswick, a name said to be derived from Sweyn, the Dane, and "wick", a village. Sweyn is said to have destroyed the pre-Norman Abbey at Bath. The church of St Mary the Virgin, with its saddleback roofed tower and its fine Norman doorway, protected by a fourteenth-century porch, contains the graves of John Wood the Elder and John Wood the Younger, the architects of Georgian Bath. In the chancel is a fine brass of a former lord of the manor, Edmund Forde of "Swayneswycke" who died in 1439. He is shown with a thin moustache turned up at the ends and he carries a short sword at his side. The brass is regarded as one of the finest examples of its period.

At Swainswick in 1600 was born William Prynne, the Puritan, who spent quite a time in prison for his views, had his ears cut off in the pillory, wrote numerous works, mostly against the church and had a chequered career in and out of Parliament. He died in Lincoln's Inn and was buried there.

Across the valley can be seen the tiny village of Woolley. In spite of their proximity to the boundary of Bath, both Swainswick and Woolley have retained a feeling of isolation in the folds of the hills and most fortunately they have avoided the fate of many villages who have lost their identities by absorption into the fringes of Bristol and Bath. When we visited Woolley there were twenty-one families centred round the little church of All Saints. Had it not been for Elizabeth Parkin, Woolley may not have had its attractive Georgian church with cupola. Having inherited

Woolley Manor, including the Woolley gunpowder mill, she visited the village from time to time and finding the church in a ruinous state, she had it rebuilt in the new style in 1761 by John Wood the Younger. Swainswick church, where he lies buried, can be seen on the hillside on the other side of the valley. In the churchyard at Woolley is the grave of Admiral Peter Puget, who died in 1822 and had sailed with Captain Vancouver on his trip round the world. His name is immortalized in Puget Sound, as is recorded on his tomb by the Seattle Historical Society.

South-east of Woolley and nearer to Bath is Charlcombe, where Henry Fielding married Charlotte Craddock in 1734. His sister, Sarah Fielding, is buried in the church. Although considerably rebuilt in 1861, the church has Norman doorways and a Norman font.

To the north-east of Charlcombe and Swainswick is St Catherine. The finest approach to the sparsely populated, scattered village is down the narrow, twisting lane from Marshfield, through one of the most scenic valleys in the county. Round one of the many bends in the road, we see before us the great manor house, standing in splendour above the lane, with its church and tithe barn. Once a priory grange of the Benedictines of Bath, the house has been altered considerably in its time, but some of its old structure still remains. A court roll shows that a manor house existed in 1310. A good part of it, including the whole of the north front, is Tudor and a Renaissance porch was added in 1610 when the terrace gardens were laid out. The undercroft, now used as a kitchen, would appear to be much older, probably part of the original priory grange and the little slip room which is now a larder may well have been a monastic cell. The property was extended in the seventeenth century, while the south-east corner of the house, incorporating the library, was built in the early twentieth century on old foundations and the orangery was added.

Following its monastic occupation, Henry VIII leased the house to Thomas Llewellyn, Rent Collector for Batheaston and afterwards granted the property to his tailor, John Malte, on condition that he adopted the King's illegitimate daughter, Ethelreda. Her marriage brought St Catherine's Court to the Harington family and, at the end of the sixteenth century, Sir John Harington, who lived at Kelston, leased and then sold it to the Blanchards. One of them incorporated his initials with those of his wife in a cornice of one of the upper rooms. In another of the upper rooms are some fine Tudor wall paintings. In fact the interior of the house is as fascinating as its exterior, with some very interesting details.

In 1841, the property passed to the Strutts who, like the Blanchards, lived there for several generations, and it is now owned by Commander and Mrs Christophers who are doing excellent work in restoring the house in keeping with its former state.

There is no village centre at St Catherine. Its farmhouses and cottages are widely scattered along the valley. St Catherine's Brook, like many of the Avon tributaries, once had its working mill, now no longer operating. There is, however, an interesting church, still used by the village. It is of late fifteenth-century date with traces of thirteenth-century work and a thirteenth-century font, but perhaps its greatest treasure is the east window of four lights, given by Prior Cantlow of Bath in the late fifteenth century, depicting the Virgin, the Crucifixion, St John and St Peter with the kneeling figure of the Prior.

The narrow road from St Catherine leads northwards back to Marshfield, a typical large Cotswold village close to Avon's eastern boundary. The name seems curious for its high, exposed position, but it has no meaning of swampy land, but of "march", a boundary. Before the advent of the motorway and the bypass, the main route from Bristol to London ran through the High Street. We remember often travelling down from London in the early hours and passing between its rows of seventeenth- and eighteenth-century houses, uniform in the grim, grey Cotswold stone, unrelieved by gardens or contrast, but if we travelled by day, the unified character of the street, in sun and shadow, gave it a very special charm.

Although the new roads have taken away much of the traffic, Marshfield has its traffic problems on Boxing Day mornings when people drive in to watch the famous "mummers' " performance by the Marshfield "paper boys" dressed in costumes of strips of paper. There is no doubt about the play's pagan origin for the old agricultural fertility cult is there, the death of winter and the rebirth of a new season, aided by "Dr Phoenix" with his dose of turpentine. The performance takes place in the Market Place at one end of the High Street and starts with carol singing, an antidote, perhaps, to pagan memories. At the end of the play, the magical seven performers, in single file, follow the "town cryer" with his yellow-banded top hat and hand bell, to the next rallying point. The members of the group are known by such names as "King William—a man of courage and bold", "Little Man John", "Old Father Belzebub", "Saucy Jack" and "Father Christmas", an historically recent addition to the mummer play.

Female players are excluded by tradition from mummer performances, but Dr Zeta Eastes told us that on one occasion a member fell ill and at the last moment, she borrowed his costume, covered her face with paper ribbons, adopted a deep Gloucestershire voice and took his place.

The play lapsed for about fifty years, but was revived in 1930, when the Reverend C. S. L. Alford heard his gardener mumbling some strange lines. His sister recognized them as part of a mummer play and searched the memories of the other elderly men of Marshfield until the performance was resurrected and takes the form seen now on Boxing Days.

The last performance is always in front of the almshouses, founded in 1619 by Elias Crispe, an interesting building with spire and gables. Close by is yet another tollhouse. One of the largest buildings in the High Street is the early eighteenth-century Catherine Wheel Inn with its attractive shell-hooded doorway. Next door is the small Tolzey Hall with the Council room on the first floor and public conveniences on the ground floor.

In the High Street is the fascinating emporium owned by Mr Bodman. In the windows are fading posters and dummy boxes of goods which have long since ceased to exist, or changed beyond recognition, while the interior is just as much a museum piece. A dress in the style of fifty years ago or more adorns a model and on the counter stands an old type of gramophone. Everywhere are mementoes from the past, including an advertisement for some wasp-waisted corsets. In fact, Mr Bodman told us that he thought he could still find a pair somewhere among the numerous drawers of the old mahogany shop fittings. He had been offered a good price for the shop by one of the large stores, but he broke off negotiations when he heard they proposed to remove the counter and change all the old fittings. The business had been established by his grandfather in 1845 and he had no desire to change it. You can still buy items at Mr Bodman's shop from biscuits to ribbons, but none of the old articles are for sale.

Marshfield is a conservation area but some new development is allowed round the perimeter of the village, in small groups of superior houses such as those at St Martin's Park. New houses are permitted to have natural or artificial slate roofs, but reroofing of old houses has to be done with the traditional Cotswold roofing stone slabs. Because of these restrictions, property is expensive, but the population has increased considerably since the war by commuters from Bath, especially from Bath University. The newcomers are particularly keen to preserve the character of the village, although opinions differ among the older inhabitants as to whether they are fully integrated into the old village life. However, changes are inevitable and Marshfield seems to be managing them pretty well.

West of Marshfield is Cold Ashton, again on the edge of the Cotswold plateau and in winter it can live up to its name. It is quite a compact village of about sixty people, mostly engaged in agriculture, but includes a few retired people and some commuters to Bristol and Bath. The nearest shops are at Marshfield, for, as is the case with many villages, Cold Ashton's village shop which was once years ago next to Shetland's Farm, has long since disappeared. Most people, with their own cars, shop weekly in Bath, only about six miles away, or even in Bristol. Shopping is more difficult for those without transport, but the infrequent bus service is augmented by a private bus service from Marshfield which makes a round of the villages and takes residents into Bath and back again.

The fine Jacobean manor house was built or rebuilt on the site of an older house about 1630. The broad stone steps leading up to the porch of the central building, flanked by two projecting wings, are glimpsed through the great ornamental gateway set in the high boundary wall. This was the home of the Gunning family. John Gunning was Mayor of Bristol, as were members of the Pepwall family who lived in the older house. For many years, the house was used as a farmhouse, but in the nineteenth century it was restored as a gentleman's residence again.

Adjoining the manor house is Church Lane leading up to the church of Holy Trinity, rebuilt by its Rector, Thomas Key, during the early part of the sixteenth century. He was so justly proud of his work that he left a reminder of himself in the form of a rebus, a key and the letter T, carved in one or two places. Fragments of the stained glass of Key's time still remain in one of the windows of the south aisle and two pieces show Key's rebus. There are memorials to the Whittington family and tombs to the north-east of the church. They were a branch of the Whittington family to which belonged Dick Whittington.

Thomas Key is said to have built the rectory on the other side of

Church Lane. It was to this building that, it is said, Sir Bevil Grenville, mortally wounded at the Battle of Lansdown, was brought to die.

Some four or five miles to the north, lies the manorial village of Dyrham. The site has its place in Saxon history, for the *Anglo-Saxon Chronicle* relates that Cuthwine and Ceawlin, the Saxon leaders, fought a great battle against the Britons and killed three of their kings. This victory secured their occupation of this part of Britain and the settlements they founded were the origins of many of our villages. The Chronicle does not tell us the exact site of the battle, but it is possible that the defences of the old Iron Age hill fort on Hinton Hill were brought into use, making this the site of the battle.

The manor house of Dyrham and its park now belong to the National Trust. In fact, some years ago, it was our privilege to complete the negotiations for the purchase of the house and its contents in connection with this acquisition. The Dennis family, who owned so many manors in the district, had a manor house there in the early sixteenth century, rebuilt from an ancient medieval house. Later in the century, the manor was purchased by the Wynter family and in the little church of Dyrham on Christmas Eve in 1686, the heiress, Mary Wynter married the gifted and ambitious William Blathwayt who was to become Secretary of State to William III. Mary was thirty-seven years old, elderly for a bride, and after five years of marriage and four children, she died and so never saw the fine house which William built after her death. The house, furniture and gardens are little changed since William Blathwayt's time and form a most interesting example of domestic life of a country gentleman at the turn of the seventeenth and during the eighteenth centuries.

From the west front, the Church Room runs towards Dyrham church and a path from the garden leads through a gate into the churchyard, It is not unusual to see a peacock from the garden perched on the church porch. The church, enlarged and restored at times, is largely of the fifteenth century, although its earliest part dates from the late thirteenth century. There are some interesting monuments of the Blathwayts, including an impressive memorial tablet to Mary and her parents and there is a spectacular tomb of Mary's great-great-grandparents, George Wynter and his wife.

The little village clusters round the church and the walled grounds of the manor house. The winding lanes and hilly ground add much to the rural character of its cottages and houses which present sixteenth- and seventeenth-century and Georgian features, including the seventeenth-century Rectory.

Across the M4, north-east of Dyrham, is Tormarton on the old Bath to Gloucester coach road near the edge of the Cotswold scarp. Behind Tormarton, running north-east and west, are miles of the undulating plateau which forms the Cotswold uplands. The long-distance footpath, the Cotswold Way, passes through the village. The old manor house stood south of St Mary Magdalene Church, but what was left of the house, including the vast kitchen and fireplace, has been incorporated into Manor Farm and the coat of arms, now well weathered, of de la Rivere, a former lord of the manor, can be seen in the end wall overlooking the churchyard. John de la Rivere was thought to have been the founder of the church because there was a brass in the church, showing the figure of de la Rivere holding a church, but it is now known that he was a benefactor and built only the south aisle in the fourteenth century. Nothing is left of the brass except the matrix which once held it. John de la Rivere established a college of priests at Tormarton and this comprised four chaplains under the jurisdiction of the rector. There is another fine brass commemorating John Ceysill, who died in 1493 and was a steward of Sir John St Loe. The heiress of the de la Rivere family married into the St Loe family.

Nearly opposite the church is the eighteenth-century Tormarton Court, formerly the rectory, almost hidden by its high stone wall. In the long main street are many interesting cottages and houses made from local Cotswold stone. Tormarton, like Marshfield and Dyrham, is a conservation area and there is little modern development.

On the other side of the A46, almost adjoining Tormarton, is Dodington with its manor house and immense park, stretching along the east side of the road as far as Cross Hands. Dodington House, with its great porticoed front, is still the home of the Codrington family and is one of the great houses in the area open to the public. James Wyatt was the architect of this magnificent house, built between 1796 and 1816 to replace the Elizabethan house which stood on the same site. Wyatt never saw his work completed for three years before the house was finished, he was killed in a carriage accident. Dodington Park is a popular place with children because of the extensive and ingenious adventure playground there. There is a carriage museum in the stables and many special exhibitions are held both in the house and the grounds. As at Dyrham, the house is connected to the church, which was rebuilt by Wyatt at the same time as the house. The church is not used by the public, only by the Codrington family on the special occasions of christenings, weddings and funerals, and for a carol service at Christmas.

Adjoining the grounds of the park is the very small village of Dodington, a manorial village still chiefly owned by the estate and occupied by the permanent staff at Dodington House on tied tenancies, with the exception of about half a dozen private residences. The tiny settlement has neither church nor shop, but both can be found at Old Sodbury, under two miles away.

The village of Old Sodbury lies to the west of the crossroads at Cross Hands. The Cross Hands Hotel was once a coaching station. This is a common name for settlements on road crossings and it is said the name comes from the time when direction signs were in the shape of a pointing hand and finger. When four hands were pointing in opposite directions, the cross roads were called the Cross Hands.

In the fields in this area can be seen small battlemented towers. These are air shafts for the two and a half miles of tunnel which runs under the hills here on the main railway line to London. This tunnel took five and a half years to complete from 1897 to 1903 and a special brickyard was established to make bricks from local clay. The number of workers added considerably to the local population. The Cross Hands Inn and the "Portcullis" at Chipping Sodbury issued 2d and 3d tokens in change which could only be used at those establishments and occasionally one of these tokens still comes to light.

The village lies a little down the hill towards Chipping Sodbury and is centred round the church of St John the Baptist. From the churchyard there are good views of the low-lying land at the foot of the Cotswolds: the spread of Yate below with the tower of Chipping Sodbury church rising beyond and, in the distance, the Somerset Tower at Hawkesbury Upton, the Nibley Tower and, in the other direction, the gleam of the Severn and the dark mass of the Welsh hills. On the Queen's Jubilee, a bonfire was lit on the hill above Old Sodbury, followed by one at Hawkesbury Upton, then by one at Chipping Sodbury and others all around. Altogether the churchyard is a pleasant place and around Easter it is yellow with daffodils.

Inside the church are two effigies in an alcove in the north transept. One is of a knight carved in wood in Bristol at the end of the fourteenth century and the other is of a knight of the thirteenth century carved in stone and nearly covered by his shield. Nobody knows whom these effigies represent but it is thought that they may have been lords of the manor. The Dog Inn in the village has an interesting Tudor doorway, while Hartley House, with its bay, was an early nineteenth-century toll gate house. However, the larger number of houses in Old Sodbury are of the post- and inter-war period, but the development is not on a large scale and the architectural styles are so varied that the modern houses blend in fairly well with the older village properties.

Just over a mile north of Old Sodbury lies Little Sodbury on the slope of the Cotswold scarp under the great Iron Age hill-fort. The manor is mostly late fifteenth century, but has been restored several times. The oldest part is its fifteenth-century hall, with an open timbered ceiling. Henry VIII and Anne Boleyn visited the manor in 1535 *en route* for Bristol when the house was owned by Sir John Walsh, Champion to Henry VIII at his Coronation, but Little Sodbury Manor is chiefly famous for the stay there between 1522 and 1523 of William Tyndale, who was later to translate the New Testament. He was chaplain and tutor to Sir John Walsh's children. Whether any of the preparatory work for his translation was done at Little Sodbury Manor, we do not know. The church was built in 1859, stands on the former village green, and is the only one in the country dedicated to St Adeline. It replaced a church of the same dedication higher up the hill near the manor house and an old gateway to the church still stands. Little Sodbury itself consists of a few scattered stone-built farmhouses and cottages.

Little more than a mile north is Horton where there is a sixteenth-century manor house, Horton Court, but the hall here is considerably older. It is Norman, a remarkable survivor of the old house, built between 1100 and 1150 as church property, although alterations have been made during the centuries. The north and south doorways of the hall are original and so are probably parts of the north wall. The timbered roof is fourteenth century. Later, the hall was divided into two floors which accounts for the eighteenth-century windows in the south wall. The upper floor was used as a Roman Catholic chapel in the eighteenth century, as a school during the nineteenth and reconverted into a hall in 1884, revealing a number of the original features.

The house itself was built in 1521 by William Knight, later

Bishop of Bath and Wells, whose arms are over the front door. He went to Italy several times on behalf of Henry VIII to try to obtain the Pope's consent to his proposal to divorce Catherine of Aragon. It was probably his liking for the architecture which he saw on these visits that led him to introduce Italian features to the house, among the earliest examples in England, such as the Renaissance porch and the ambulatory or covered walk detached from the house. The house was much restored in 1937 and is now the property of the National Trust, although only the hall is open to the public.

The church of St James is next to the manor house and, although restored in 1865, it still retains some fourteenth-fifteenth- and sixteenth-century details. The gabled national school of 1860 with its decorated chimneys and bellcote still stands, on a slope above the road to Horton Court and the church. P. A. Couzens, in his book *The Sodburys*, mentions a past custom of Horton known as the "Horton Bull", when at Christmas time, villagers from Horton used to bring the skin and horns of a bull and parade with it in the public bars in Chipping Sodbury as part of the carol and wassailing festivities.

A short way north of Horton is Hawkesbury. The village is in two parts. The church of St Mary the Virgin, the old parsonage, a farmhouse with farm buildings and cottage, all that remains of a once flourishing village, clusters below the hill, while the upland village of Hawkesbury Upton is up the hill on the edge of the escarpment. The approach from Wickwar is the most attractive, across South Moon Ridings and Inglestone Common with nearby woods famed for nightingales, then up to the Somerset Monument on the crest of the hill. This great tower was erected in 1846 to the memory of Lord Robert Edward Henry Somerset of the Beaufort family of Badminton, about three miles away. He fought at Waterloo and a tablet just inside the door tells us of his background and career. The 145 steps bring us to a magnificent view from all quarters. In one direction you can see the thin shining line of the Severn, in another the rolling top of the Cotswolds and in yet another, the rooftops of Hawkesbury Upton below.

Hawkesbury Upton is still a Cotswold village strung along its main street with grey stone houses, some Georgian and some Victorian, including the village school and adjoining small church. The inn signs remind us that this is hunting country. The sign at the Duke of Beaufort public house shows the Duke in hunting kit and on the other side of the street is the Fox Inn, with the sign of a fox with a goose in his mouth. There are some lanes leading off the main street with some old and modern houses, including a very fine one in Georgian style at the top of Back Street. There is a special quality about Hawkesbury Upton and the villages on the plateau. They seem bleak, remote and unchanging and because of this, have well-knit village communities. Certain of them need some development of small-scale local industry to provide employment and so maintain well-balanced communities in the villages and in the surrounding districts. The planning authorities recognize this, but such development may bring changes.

A very steep lane leads down the escarpment to Hawkesbury itself and soon the great church comes into view, out of all proportion to the tiny hamlet. Opposite the church was a manor house which fell into ruins and was pulled down in the nineteenth century. It is said that the Jenkins family abandoned the house because of two family tragedies. A daughter of Sir Robert Jenkins, who lived there in the seventeenth century, fell in love with one of the Pastons, the Catholic family at Horton Court, but being a staunch Protestant, Sir Robert forbade the match. As his daughter was waving goodbye to young Paston, she fell to her death from an oriel window. The family then moved out of the house, but later, in the eighteenth century, the 6th Baronet lent the house to his cousin Charles who was to bring his young wife there after the birth of their son. She died on the journey and her body was brought to the manor for burial in the local church. The house was then abandoned and eventually fell into ruins. The son became Prime Minister following the assassination of the Prime Minister Spencer Percival in 1812.

Hanging in the porch of the church is a pair of old pattens, once worn by women on their way to church to keep their feet clear of the mud. Women left their pattens in the porch to comply with the notice desiring that all people would "leave their Dogs at home and that the Women would not walk in with their Pattens on". The interior of the church appears almost cathedral like in its size and in the Middle Ages, it served a very large and wealthy parish. It is mainly Perpendicular in style, but there is some Norman and Decorated work, while the chancel is mostly Early English. Like most of our churches it was restored in the nineteenth century, but not drastically so. Into the base of the fifteenth-century pulpit is incorporated a piece of Saxon stone, interlaced work no doubt from a Saxon church which once stood on the site. Traces of this ancient church are believed to have been found when excavations were made in the late nineteenth century for the installation of a new heating system.

Of all the incumbents at Hawkesbury, by far the most famous was St Wulfstan, who was at Hawkesbury at some time between 1033 and 1038 and later became Bishop of Worcester. In spite of the Norman Conquest, he retained his office until after William I's death. He died in 1095 and is buried in Worcester Cathedral. Next to the church is the old vicarage with its fine fifteenth-century front. It is now a private house and the present vicar has a house in Hawkesbury Upton. We were told by the lady who owns it that it was not too large because it was spared the usual Victorian extensions, since by that time, Hawkesbury had already declined.

Just south-east of Hawkesbury are Dunkirk and Petty France. Their names are a bit of a mystery. They certainly have no connection with the Napoleonic Wars, as both names appear in the Hawkesbury rate books in the eighteenth century and Dunkirk is recorded as early as 1706. It has been suggested that the names may refer to a continental weaver settlement, although these are usually of Flemish origin. Dunkirk has no village except for a few farm buildings, but Petty France has one or two interesting houses in the vicinity of the old inn, now an attractive restaurant of that name built about 1777 and believed to be the building to which Jane Austen referred in her *Mansfield Park*. There was an inn at Petty France at least as early as 1740, catering for coaching passengers. At the crossroads at Dunkirk, the Turnpike Trust had a toll house and the barrier there was known as "Dunkirk Gates".

A mile and a half north of Dunkirk is the hamlet of Upper Kilcott, with two prehistoric burial mounds, one each side of the A46. A lane runs from Upper to Lower Kilcott by the side of a stream where there are several old mills, mostly converted to houses. One particularly interesting converted mill has its mill pond. We pass through these hamlets almost without noticing them and continue to the village of Hillesley, following the stream and its deep wooded valley for most of the way.

The church of St Giles at Hillesley was built in 1851 to the design of the Reverend Benjamin Perkins, for during this period of church restoration and building, many of the clergy turned amateur architects. Hillesley Farmhouse is a seventeenth-century gabled building, while Yew Tree House bears a date of 1701. The public house is "The Fleece", a reminder of the days when the Cotswolds were a great wool area. Hillesley is not a Cotswold show village. It has the atmosphere of a working village with some very large and sometimes ugly farm buildings and certain modern development.

Tresham, to the north-east, is a typical Cotswold scarp hamlet in the north-east corner of the county. It has no true centre, only a scattering of old stone houses with stone slab roofs. Here and there a new house has been built in the appropriate Cotswold style. Footpaths lead from the hamlet down steep valleys to Hillesley and the Kilcotts and everywhere there are splendid views.

To the south-east of Hawkesbury is Badminton, one of the most well-known names in the Cotswold fringe area, for Badminton Park, the seat of the Duke of Beaufort, is famous for the Badminton Horse Trials in April and is often visited by members of the Royal Family. The house was built for Henry, 3rd Marquess of Worcester and 1st Duke of Beaufort, but was re-modelled and enlarged by William Kent for the 3rd Duke about 1746. William Kent also designed Worcester Lodge, a spectacular gateway on the northern boundary of the park, where the Beaufort Hunt meet on Boxing Day morning. On these occasions there is always a crowd to watch the riders and hounds depart. In the entrance hall of the house, a former duke and his family were supposed to have invented the game of badminton using shuttle-cocks instead of tennis balls to avoid damaging the pictures which are a feature of this room. The game does appear to have originated in India, but was probably first played in this country at Badminton.

The house has a private entrance to the church of St Michael and All Angels, which is also the church for the village of Great Badminton and the surrounding area. The church was built in 1785 as a miniature of St Martin's in the Fields, except for the tower. The chancel was added in 1875 to accommodate the 25-foot-high monument by Grinling Gibbons to Henry Somerset, the 1st Duke, who died in 1699. The monument was originally at Windsor. There are many Beaufort memorials in the church, one to the 1st Duchess and one to the 2nd Duke, showing him reclining in Roman dress and his son Henry standing at his side. Among other monuments is that to Lord Robert Edward Henry Somerset, whose monumental tower is at Hawkesbury Upton.

The village is essentially an estate village with houses of

various dates bordering a wide road and it is a charming addition to the great house and park. The fine row of almshouses dates to about 1714 and there is no doubt about the houses' patronage, as they display the ducal arms and were founded by the 1st Duchess. Essex House dates to the early eighteenth century. There is no public house at Badminton, but instead there is a club for the inhabitants.

Not far from Great Badminton is Little Badminton with its medieval dovecot, standing in the middle of the village green. The church of St Michael adjoining the green is of twelfth-century origin. Some of the cottages have thatched roofs, not common in the Cotswolds, where the traditional roofing is in stone, but thatched roofs are one of the features of the Badminton Park estate. Ornate Gothic-type thatched cottages can be seen on the way from Great Badminton to Acton Turville.

The influence of the Beauforts is still apparent at Acton Turville by their badge, a portcullis, which appears on the roof of the canopied well on the small green. This is reputed to have been the site of a sanctuary dating back to the Saxon period. The church of St Mary was rebuilt in the nineteenth century, but still retains relics from the old church, including a Norman font and interesting thirteenth-century bellcote. This, again, is a village, chiefly of the grey local Cotswold stone. At one end of the main street, opposite the Fox and Hounds Inn, is an interesting early nineteenth-century toll-house which has survived from the days of the turnpike roads.

7

South and South-West of Bath

The outlying hills of the Cotswolds and the Mendips meet to the south and south-west of Bath and merge to form a green undulating landscape of low hills, valleys and narrow winding lanes, bordered by hedgerows, in contrast to the upper plateaux, with their wide open fields and heathland bounded by dry stone walling. The land here is sheltered compared to the exposed uplands and we have often driven from Wells across the Mendips or over the Cotswolds in mist or snow to descend to the lowland area to find the weather clear and frost free.

Just outside the south-west boundary of Bath is Englishcombe, one of the many quiet villages on the edge of that busy city, quiet except for the occasional sortie of the village youths on their motorcycles and the children playing round the door of the small post office and sweet shop. The south-western edge of Bath can just be seen on the ridge which carries the road from Newton St Loe to Odd Down, a fairly busy road, but just too far away to disturb the rural setting of Englishcombe. The village is reputed to have once been the seat of Saxon kings and the Wansdyke, the great boundary bank, built in Saxon times, passes near the churchyard. Once a continuous line of defence, only parts of it remain in the county. Stretches are to be seen south of Newton Park, adjoining the Iron Age hill fort on Stantonbury Hill, near Compton Dando, and at Maes Knoll. Its course across the county can easily be traced on a large-scale Ordnance Survey map.

In spite of its proximity to the housing estates on the edge of Bath, there is little new in Englishcombe. It is a village of mostly old houses, cottages, farms and a delightful church which has quite a lot of Norman work. Along the top of the exterior chancel wall is a Norman corbel table, carved with amusing faces, and inside there are even more interesting carvings. On the north side of the chancel, a capital has a carved grotesque face with horse-like teeth and is thought by some to represent the devil. There is a curious figure of a child in swaddling clothes on the altar side at the top of the chancel arch. This could have come from a family tomb, but it is thought by others to represent the "Bambino" or the Christ Child. Adjoining the chancel arch and forming the north side of the tower are the remains of a Norman arcade. Between the porch and the south chapel are two bell-shaped squints with consecration crosses, which some sources suggest were carved by pilgrims.

The south chapel was erected by the de Gournays in the early thirteenth century. Once lords of the manor, they lived in Culverhay Castle, of which little remains of the supporting mound, not far from the church. In 1279, Anselm de Gournay was summoned for possessing gallows, pillory, tumbril and for exercising certain manorial rights which, he claimed, had always been the prerogative of the de Gournays. Thomas de Gournay was implicated in the murder of Edward II in 1327 and eventually forfeited his estates to the Crown. Englishcombe is now part of the Duchy of Cornwall's vast domain. The church has quite a display of standards. A churchwarden and his wife whom we met in the church told us that at the end of the Second World War, it was decided to ask the various services for a flag to commemorate the villagers who had served with them during the war. As a result there are now in the church flags from the R.A.F., the Royal Navy, the R.N.V.R., the Merchant Navy and, to represent the army, Montgomery's own flag.

South-west of Englishcombe is Priston, which is quite a small, pretty village with a church almost dwarfed by its enormous weathercock. One story is that a benefactor gave some money for a church clock, but the cost of the clock was far less than the money donated, so a weathercock was ordered for "one of the tallest towers in England", a statement far from the truth. When the huge weathercock arrived, it was filled with beer and when that had been consumed, it was hoisted, somewhat unsteadily one would imagine, to the top of the tower. Another explanation is that it was erected in 1813 by William Vaughan, the lord of the manor, to satisfy his vanity by making as conspicuous a gift as possible. The church has Norman work, but much of the Norman and some of the later styles are the result of extensive restoration in the nineteenth century. An interesting feature is the heavy medieval studded wooden south door with its enormous iron hinges.

A prominent building in the village is the village hall. Thought to have been originally a barn, it was converted into the Parish Poor House and from 1838 to 1970, it was the village school. By 1978, the building had reached almost a state of collapse, but through fund-raising efforts, a Government grant and the voluntary work of certain residents, it was put back into order as a village hall. It has been suggested that Priston's name is derived from "Priests' Town", no doubt because it was once part of the Bath Abbey estates.

Not far from the village is Priston Mill, an old corn mill complete with a 25-foot diameter overshot water wheel and still grinding corn with its old equipment, augmented now by electrical power. It is open to the public, but it is no museum, for its products, wholewheat stone-ground flour, porridge oats and bran, are sold commercially far and wide.

Travelling east from Priston through the winding lanes and crossing the main road from Bath to Radstock, we come to the pretty village of Combe Hay in a deep valley with old ochre-coloured stone houses, free from modern development, and the fifteenth-century church tower rises above the screen of trees in the grounds of the adjoining eighteenth-century manor house. When we were at Combe Hay one autumn day, two little girls and one boy came along the village street. The small boy had been given the dolls to carry and the girls were pushing the dolls' pram filled with the largest puff balls we had ever seen. The children had collected them and were distributing them around the village. They gave us one which made a very agreeable addition to our breakfasts for a couple of days.

That afternoon, with the autumn sunshine mellowing the stone, Combe Hay was a perfect example of rural England, but at the beginning of the nineteenth century, the area was a centre of activity in an attempt to solve one of the most difficult problems of canal construction. In 1794, an Act of Parliament was passed for the construction of a canal to link the Kennet and Avon Canal with the Somerset Coalfield. The problem was the considerable gradient at Combe Hay. It was decided on a scheme to lift and lower boats forty-five feet within a caisson. The caisson was a failure and William Smith, "Strata Smith" to his associates, the father of English geology, who was the engineer in charge of the works, was dismissed. The caisson was replaced by an inclined plane, but this was a lengthy procedure and had to be replaced in its turn by a flight of traditional locks, which can still be seen.

The canal prospered for a long time, but like many canals, it lost its trade to the railways, became derelict and now attracts only the industrial historian. Its filled-in junction with the Kennet and Avon Canal can still be seen by the disused wharf at the bend by the great Dundas aqueduct near Limpley Stoke. The filled-in junction now forms part of the garden of a house and the stone edges of the canal can be seen above the grass. The canal was abandoned in 1898 and the Camerton to Limpley Stoke railway line laid, part of it in the dried-out canal bed, with halts at Combe Hay and Dunkerton colliery.

Dunkerton, once a colliery village, is not far to the west of Combe Hay and was close to the Somerset Coal Canal. It was quite usual on many of the canals and rivers to use a commercial vessel for an annual works or private outing, all suitably cleaned up and decorated with bunting for the occasion. In his diary, the Reverend Skinner of Camerton records an outing he made in June 1822 with his private party from Camerton through Dunkerton to Combe Hay and he tells us that on the return journey, when passing "The Swan" at Dunkerton, the Camerton band came aboard and they "played marches and Scotch airs the whole way home".

From Combe Hay, we travel a mile eastwards along the narrow road and then northwards towards Bath up the steep Hodshill. In under a mile we come to South Stoke, another pretty village, built mostly in Bath stone and with one of the most interesting old pubs we know, the Packhorse Inn. The name appears to have been given to the building in 1825, when the old packhorse trail was replaced by the road passing right in front of the inn. No doubt the packhorse drivers needed a drink after leading their animals up the steep hill. Before that date, the inn seems to have been at Packhorse Farm, but probably the present inn served and sold beer long before it became officially an inn. The present family took over the licence in 1888 and have been there ever since. The gabled stone building was erected in 1674, a rebuilding of an older house which stood on the site and probably incorporating some of the older structure. Some of the mullioned windows, including two in the front gables, are blocked in, reminders of the window tax introduced in 1697 and repealed in

1851. A tax was payable on each window, so householders would reduce their liability by reducing the number of their windows.

A tunnel, long since blocked, is supposed to connect the Pack-horse Inn with the church, but it cannot now be found. Another way to the church is through the central passage, now no longer a right of way. Coffins used to be carried this way to the church from the Packhorse Cottages on the opposite side of the road and a stay would be made while the bearers quenched their thirst with money left by the deceased for that purpose. The inside of the inn is as old and unspoilt as the outside, amazingly so for its proximity to the city. There are stone slab floors, open fireplaces, and beautifully carved old settles. Shove ha'penny boards lie on the tables and traditional ale and draught cider is sold, although now produced commercially.

The garden path behind the pub takes a short cut to the church, although like the way round by road it climbs steeply for South Stoke is built on a hilly slope, which adds to its charm. The only Norman evidence of St James the Great is the north doorway. The tower is of the early sixteenth century, but much of the remainder of the church was rebuilt in 1712, but restored again in the mid nineteenth century, when the chancel was rebuilt and the south aisle added. Manor Farm is another fine old building of similar age and design as the Packhorse Inn and has an even earlier barn and dovecot.

A road south through Midford comes to the village of Hinton Charterhouse, but for the name and history of the village, we have to go a mile or so north-east to the remains of Hinton Priory, just off the A36. The Carthusian order of monks gave the name of Charterhouse to their monastic settlements and here the second Carthusian house to be founded in England was established in 1232. All that remain are the chapter house, with library and dovecot above, the refectory, now used as a barn and the outline of the cloister. The chapter house has some fine examples of carving and ancient tiles and, although the barn contains but the bare walls of the refectory, it has an interesting vaulted under-croft. On one occasion, we arrived at the same time as a twenty-fifth wedding anniversary party. The guests almost filled the chapter house and the visit to the library and pigeon loft was somewhat prolonged as only six were allowed at a time up the narrow staircase. The gatehouse and guesthouse, or parts of them, were incorporated in the house built by the Hungerfords in the late sixteenth century. During excavations in 1950, the owner of the property, Major P. C. Fletcher, uncovered remains of two of the monks' dwellings adjoining the main cloister, a small cloister and part of the monastic church. Major Fletcher noticed that a doorway cill of one of the monks' dwellings would fit a bedroom door in the house, so a considerable amount of material on the monastic site may have been used in the construction of the house. Each monk occupied his own dwelling round the cloister, while the lay brothers lived about three quarters of a mile away where Friary Wood now stands, as indeed was usual in early Carthusian settlements.

The village of Hinton Charterhouse, a mile to the south-west, has its street of stone houses, some with mullioned windows, by the church of St John the Baptist and a further settlement along by the crossroads. There is some modern development, but not enough to change the character of the village. The church was founded in Norman times and the south doorway and the font remain from this period, while the lower part of the tower is probably late Norman, so the church was already there when the Priory was founded by the Countess of Salisbury. The advowson or right of patronage of the church was given to the Priory and was the subject of dispute between the Prior and the Rector for a time. In the churchyard, we came upon a plaque on a wooden seat with this inscription: "This seat contains teak from H.M. Ship 'Valiant' Jutland 1916. Cape Matapan 1941". Nearby is Hinton House with its pleasing façade of 1701.

To the west of Hinton Charterhouse is Wellow, where down a steep village street is a ford by a medieval packhorse bridge across the Wellow Brook. Here you can lean on the bridge and watch the few cars ploughing slowly through the water below. Behind the bridge is the old mill, now a dwelling, Climbing the hill again to High Street, you will see the old thirteenth-century dovecot of the Manor, a fine circular building, the purpose of which was to provide pigeon meat for the manorial table during the winter scarcity. In the main street is the Wellow National School built in 1852, some interesting old houses and a raised pavement reminiscent of the causeway at Chew Magna.

The church of St Julian is reputed to have been built in the fourteenth century by Sir Thomas Hungerford, lord of the manor, some believe on the site of an earlier church, and, except for the rebuilding of the chancel in the nineteenth century, it has been little changed. Collinson, in his *History of Somerset* of 1791, records that there had been some murals in the Hungerford

Chapel, but they had been destroyed. When the old organ was removed in 1951, faint outlines were seen on the wall and the plaster was removed, revealing the wall paintings of about 1500 that we see today of Christ with the twelve Apostles, probably the only church wall murals of this subject in the country. Opposite the church is Church Farm House, a fine seventeenth-century building.

Between Wellow and Shoscombe at Stoney Littleton is one of the finest restored Neolithic chambered tombs in Britain, where people buried their dead nearly four thousand years ago. It is a pleasant walk either from Wellow or from Stoney Littleton, but the key is kept at Stoney Littleton farm.

On a slope above the Wellow Brook with some new houses mingling with the old, is Shoscombe on the border of the county. It has no church, but an inn, the "Apple Tree", which is appropriate as the area has many small orchards. Paglinch Farmhouse at Shoscombe Bottom was built in 1632.

Within a short distance of Shoscombe is Peasedown St John. Like many other places in the area, it was once a mining village, for it had its own Braysdown Colliery and the deepest pit in the Somerset Coal Field in 1817 was at Clandown, only a short distance away. Today there is very little to be seen of the once thriving industry which expanded so enormously in the nineteenth century and gradually declined in the twentieth with pit closures until the last colliery closed at Kilmersdon in 1969, As a mining village, Peasedown St John grew rapidly with the expansion of the industry and the church of St John was built in 1892-4 to serve the increased population. With the closure of the pits, many villages in the area dwindled, or reverted to their rural state, but others like Peasedown St John, because of their proximity to Bath and Radstock, had a second lease of life as commuter villages with quite considerable modern development.

There are two interesting inns at Peasedown St John, the "Red Post" and the "Waggon and Horses". The "Red Post" is mentioned a number of times in the early nineteenth-century diaries of the Reverend Skinner of Camerton. He complained to the squire about the drunkenness and riots which went on there and also says that one of his parishioners "died of a consumption brought on in a great measure by excessive drinking" at the "Red Post". The "Red Post" was not the only inn of which he complained and it is obvious from his diaries that he had two great dislikes, drinkers and Methodists. The "Waggon and Horses" has a different story. It is reputed to have been haunted by a man in black who appeared at the unearthly hours of 2 or 3 a.m. Umbrellas and crates have been thrown about, things moved and hidden and he has even interfered with the beer gas pressures.

Peasedown St John lies in an area between two streams, the Wellow and the Cam Brooks, which rise on the northern slopes of the Mendips. They later join at Midford and finally merge with the Avon near Limpley Stoke. On the Cam is Camerton. One of its landmarks is the huge slag heap which once marred the landscape, but now, with its cover of grass and trees, has the appearance of a great conical hill. Like Peasedown St John, Camerton was once a colliery village, but the Camerton Colliery closed in 1950 and the Limpley Stoke to Hallatrow railway line which served Camerton and a number of other collieries closed less than a year later. The railway had a very brief respite in 1953 when film sequences for *The Titfield Thunderbolt* were taken. Today, Camerton is mainly an agricultural village and a residential area. We know a great deal about life in Camerton and the surrounding district in the early nineteenth century from John Skinner, who was rector there and bequeathed his diaries to the British Museum, in spite of the remarks of his son Joseph who told him that no one would ever read his works. He was also interested in local antiquities, an interest so keenly followed in our own times by the Camerton Excavation Club, under the direction of Mr W. J. Wedlake, that much information about the archaeology of Camerton has come to light.

As well as in other churches in the neighbourhood, Skinner, of course, preached at Camerton at St Peter's, with its Carew chapel containing elaborate tombs of the Carew family, who were lords of the manor from 1584-1750. In their time, the Manor House adjoined the church, but in 1835, it was replaced by Camerton Court, an imposing house, with colonnaded portico, separated from the church by attractive rising lawns and gardens. A fine view of the house is seen from the churchyard, entered from the grounds by a little private gate. Unlike the house, the church is in a hollow and, from certain angles, is almost hidden, creating an atmosphere of quietness and seclusion. On one of the plaques on the outside of the north porch is the following inscription:

Come hither mortal cast an eye
Then go thy way prepared to die
Read here thy doom for know thou must
One day like me be turned to dust

Across the valley, but still in Camerton is "The Jolly Collier", said to have been the Camerton Inn of Skinner's day. On its forecourt is a large fibreglass model of a collier, a copy of a bronze statue made for the National Coal Board for the Festival of Britain. It is a reminder of the time when Camerton was a colliery village and its now quiet and rural roads echoed to the ring of the miners' boots to and from the Camerton Mine and the Reverend Skinner had cause to complain bitterly of their ribaldry at the "Red Post" and the Camerton Inn.

Closely associated with Camerton is Clandown, for both produced good bituminous coal in the mining days. The church was built in 1849 to serve the growing mining population.

Almost rubbing shoulders with Clandown is Radstock, which, with its twin town Midsomer Norton, formed the focal point of the Somerset Coalfield. Neither are villages, but small industrial towns and have remained so, in spite of the closure of the Somerset Coalfield. The two towns form the area of Norton-Radstock and, although it is difficult to distinguish where Radstock ends and Midsomer Norton begins, they are each conscious of their individuality. Unlike neighbouring colliery villages which reverted to their rural states, Radstock and particularly Midsomer Norton, developed other industries from engineering to bread making. A flexible packaging factory, at Norton Hill, just outside Midsomer Norton, has the largest and probably one of the most modern roof spans in England. Other industries include shoe making, printing, animal feeds, machine making, stationery and zinc and aluminium processing. With industry have grown large housing estates, particularly at Midsomer Norton and Westfield, where many acres of land are zoned for small factories, the developing bridging area between Midsomer Norton and Radstock.

St Michael's Church at Radstock is an 1879 rebuilding, incorporating the tower, south wall and porch of an older church, and that at Midsomer Norton, St John the Baptist, is an 1830 building, retaining its seventeenth-century tower with a figure believed to be Charles II in a niche on the tower wall. In the churchyard is the communal grave of twelve men and boys, the youngest only twelve years old, killed in the Wellsway Pit at Radstock in 1839 when the hauling rope broke during the descent, hurtling them to the bottom of the 756-feet-deep shaft. According to the grave inscription, "the rope was generally supposed to have been maliciously cut", although some thought that the rope had been damaged by catching in the cog wheels. It was not the only disaster of its kind in the area, for a rope snapped at Paulton Engine Pit in 1830 during the ascent at 50 feet above the pit bottom. Of the nine men and boys, four men and a boy were killed, and the Reverend Skinner relates in his diary: "There could not have been less than 1,000 people who attended the funeral." There were no pit cages in the area before 1850. Most of the shafts were only about 4 feet 6 inches across and the usual method of descending or ascending was by a "hudge" in which the coal was hauled to the surface, especially adapted for human transport by a covered top as a protection against falling stones. Its capacity was limited and more men and boys could be carried by the "hooker" method. Each miner had a looped rope which went round his thigh and a hook on the rope was put into one of the links of a chain at the end of the hauling rope. In this way about a dozen miners strung along the chain could be hauled up or lowered. Each held on by one hand, leaving the other free to ward off the sides of the narrow shaft.

The central area of Midsomer Norton is called "The Island" and on the corner is the Town Hall built in 1860 in Italianate style, with its wide overhanging eaves, more suitable, no doubt, for sheltering the building from the Italian sun than that of Midsomer Norton. One of the most interesting buildings in the whole of Norton-Radstock is the Catholic church of the Holy Ghost, for it is a converted fifteenth-century tithe barn which once belonged to the Augustinian Canons of Merton Priory in Surrey. Since the Dissolution, it had a chequered career, including its use as kennels, a stable and even as a chicken house. It was purchased by Downside Abbey in 1906 and, after removing the various outbuildings and excrescences it had acquired during the ages, it was transformed back to its original form to house the church. The first Mass was held in 1913.

A short distance behind "The Island", within a pleasant tiny park, close to the millhouse, a small spring joins the River Somer. This is St Chad's Well. Over it is an obelisk, erected more than a hundred years ago by Lady Savage in memory of her son Frederick, a "major of the 86th Regiment formerly of the 68th Light Infantry in which regiment he served throughout the Crimean Campaign and received for his services the Crimean and Sebastapol Medal". He died in 1866. In 1979, the spring dried up during the time the Wessex Water Authority were carrying out some tunnelling work and was the subject of a furore amongst

some of Midsomer Norton's residents. The River Somer flows
along the High Street and one day we asked a small boy and girl,
wading along the stream with fishing nets, what they were
looking for. "Minnows," replied the boy, and sure enough, there
were many small fish darting in and out of the long flowing
weeds. Although it is said that Midsomer Norton owes its first
name to the River Somer, this is doubtful and it is claimed that
the name is derived from a midsummer festival once held there.
John Wesley suggested that the town was so named because it
was only approachable in the summer owing of the state of the
roads.

Paulton was at one time a colliery village of some importance,
but its chief industry now is the vast Purnell printing works. As at
many other villages in the Radstock-Norton area, Paulton's older
buildings are of the thin-banded limestones from shallow
quarries in the district. In 1832, there was an epidemic of Asiatic
cholera at Paulton and a grim reminder of this is an inscription in
the churchyard: "In memory of 23 men, 23 women and 26
children interred within this enclosure who fell victim to that
dreadful scourge Asiatic Cholera with which it pleased the
Almighty to visit the Parish on the 28th September to the 10th
November 1832 when under the directing arm of a bountiful
providence by the skill and attention of the medical men and by
the charitable donations of the surrounding neighbourhood it
ceased." At the bottom are the words: "And he stood between
the living and the dead and the plague was stayed." The inscription was restored in 1966.

The outbreak occurred during the time the Reverend John
Skinner was rector at Camerton, which also suffered. Among the
references in his diary to the plague he stated in his entry of 11th
October 1832: "I hear that nearly forty persons have died of the
cholera at Paulton and that they are interred without funeral
service." The villagers were probably worried that the priest
would contract the plague during the funeral. Skinner himself
was advised not to officiate at a burial of a cholera victim, but
insisted on doing so and was one of those who escaped the
disease. The church of the Holy Trinity has a tower of 1757 and
over the porch is the date 1839, when the remainder of the church
was rebuilt by John Pinch, who restored St John the Baptist
Church at Midsomer Norton.

Hallatrow, just outside Paulton and beside the Cam, was called
in the Domesday Book Helgetreu, which in Saxon meant "Holy

tree". Was there ever a holy tree and if so, was this a meeting place for the Saxons?

Across the A39 from Hallatrow and a couple of miles to the north-west is Clutton, where coal was being worked as far back as 1610 but as elsewhere in the old Somerset Coalfield, the industry no longer exists. Like many villages, Clutton has more than one centre, one round the church, another round the Railway Hotel and yet another on the main road, the A37. The church is dedicated to St Augustine and has been much restored including the twelfth-century doorway and chancel arch. The reddish sandstone tower dates from the eighteenth century and near the church are several modernized old cottages.

Back on the A39, a mile north of Hallatrow, we find another old mining village once with its own mine, the village of High Littleton. As its name implies, it stands comparatively high for these parts, a little over 500 feet, with extensive views of the surrounding countryside. The church of Holy Trinity was rebuilt in 1885 but the late fourteenth-century tower was retained. The earlier church was one of those that came into the possession of Keynsham Abbey and remained with the Abbey until the Dissolution. Two interesting houses are High Littleton House of about 1710 and Pembroke House of 1777.

Timsbury, a little to the north, was yet another mining village, but has little to show of its once thriving industry. In common with other villages in the area, there is still a hint of industrialization about it, perhaps in the miners' cottages, where they once lived in far more primitive conditions than do the present-day commuters. Then, too, there is usually the sight of old slag heaps, but Nature, with human help, is doing her best to diminish them with grass and trees and to obliterate the remains of the old engine houses and the like with a covering of weeds and shrubs. Even the pubs, like the "Guss and Crook", bearing the date of 1703, and the ancient but undated "Seven Stars", have an air of tranquillity. Except for the weekend visitors, locals stroll in and out and life seems leisurely enough where once there must have been the vigorous life of the mining community. In fact, the landlord of the "Seven Stars" told us that in the mining days there were several inns in Timsbury, but the others had closed when the pits shut down.

The name "Guss and Crook" was the term for the harness by which the colliery boys pulled the laden sledges or "puts" to the base of the shaft. The "guss" was a leather or rope belt round the

boy's waist from which a chain or "tugger" was attached to the
"put" by a hook or crook. On the wall of the "Seven Stars" is a
painting of a large house, of which only the lodge survives today.
When we were last there, it was being used as an office for the
contractors who were building houses on the site of the demolished house. The village has some interesting eighteenth-century
houses and part of Timsbury is a conservation area, but the
church was rebuilt in 1826, and the chancel added in 1852.

Under two miles to the north of Timsbury is Farmborough,
where there are quite a number of between-the-wars houses and
others recently built, while the older area lies off the main road.
When driving through the countryside, the motorist often misses
the main part of a village. He may see some modern development, an old coaching inn or two and catch a glimpse of a spire
some way off through the trees, but the church and the centre of
the village is often some way off the road. Farmborough is such a
village. At the bottom of a hill, past the church, the village street
follows a stream, deeply cut beside the road and bridged over at
intervals to serve the houses on the other side. The church,
except for its Perpendicular tower, has been largely rebuilt.
Farmborough, like Timsbury, is a village within the old coal-
mining area. To replace the loss of the mining industry, other
industry is being encouraged, together with accompanying
housing development.

From Farmborough a minor road cuts through to the A368 and
a couple of miles to the west along this road is the little village of
Chelwood, where coal was mined from an early date until the
early nineteenth century. St Leonard's Church is approached by
a narrow lane lined with cottages, a pretty rural scene. The
church is mainly nineteenth century, but the tower was rebuilt in
1772. Like many churches, it has a Norman font and it is interesting to note how many Norman fonts have survived church
rebuildings. At each end of the nave's south arcade are corbels
believed to be fourteenth century. Both are foliated. That at the
east has a female face incorporated with vine leaves, while that at
the west is purely a foliation of fig leaves. The windows parallel
with this arcade have inserts of Flemish glass of the sixteenth
century. The village is mentioned in the Domesday Book, but its
record goes back even earlier, to 925, when a villager Robert le
Bok was acquitted of arson in connection with a house belonging
to John de Kylkenny.

Under three miles to the east is the junction of the A368 and the

A39 roads and just north of the junction is Marksbury, conspicuous before you enter it by the snub tower of St Peter's Church, with its oversize corner pinnacles, each crowned with its own weathervane, a fourfold confirmation of the direction of the wind. Marksbury is believed to have derived its name from *merc*, an Old English word meaning frontier, perhaps connected with that great frontier of bank and ditch, the Wansdyke, which skirts the Early Iron Age hill fort on nearby Stantonbury Hill. There have been some modern houses built at Marksbury, but in a style conforming with the older stone houses of the village, although occasionally old buildings, including the turnpike cottage, have been pulled down to make way for the new. Some of the cottages are eighteenth century, although in the seventeenth-century architectural style, which lingered on in spite of the new trend.

Just outside Marksbury is Hunstrete, a hamlet of stone houses, some modernized. Hunstrete House, a large early Victorian mansion, has an early Georgian door pediment. This came from an earlier house which once stood by the lake in the grounds. The present house is now a hotel and restaurant and the lake is used by the Bathampton Anglers' Association.

A mile from Marksbury is Stanton Prior, part of the estates of the Priory at Bath until the Dissolution. The arms of Bath Abbey still remain on a boss in the local church of St Lawrence. The church, basically thirteenth century, was much restored in 1860, but still has its thirteenth-century north porch and probably thirteenth-century south doorway, while the fifteenth-century tower remains. In the church is an interesting memorial to Thomas Cox who died in 1650. It is a wall monument with the effigies of Thomas Cox and his wife leaning on either side of a table where rests a skull. The wife is holding a baby and the memorial shows their other children, including a son and a daughter with skulls at their feet to tell us that they had died before the monument was erected. The inscription, defaced and difficult to read, is as follows:

> Christ is our head, our hope, our life, and wee
> His members live in Him, though dead wee bee
> He died for sinne, sinners to free from paine
> His die to save and rise with him again.
>
> "Thomas Cox Feb. 28th 1650

There was a tradition that an ancient yew in the churchyard marked the communal grave of victims of the Black Death. The story was not generally accepted, but a grave digger found, among the roots of the tree, a number of skeletons. A framed newspaper page of 16th February 1932 in the church deplores the depopulation of the village. It states that about fifty years previously the population was about 126, but because of agricultural decline and its replacement by the milk industry which required fewer labourers, the population in 1932 was only 60. Today, of course, with further mechanization and improvements in farm management, the need for manual labourers has become even less, but now their empty cottages are quickly snapped up by commuters. Stanton Prior, with its old church and stone-built cottages and farmhouses and little or no modern development is an idyllic village and many people would like to live there, for we are near Bath now and the Avon and Chew Valleys.

Some three miles to the north-west is the hamlet of Burnett, within sight of the Chew Valley. The little church of St Michael has an interesting brass to John Cutte who died in 1575, his wife, eight sons and four daughters. He had been Mayor of Bristol. It was another Mayor of Bristol connected with Burnett, John Whitson, who gave Bristol one of its most important educational establishments. When he died in 1628, he bequeathed an annuity from the manor of Burnett to the City for the foundation of a school for forty poor girls. A condition of the bequest was that the girls should be dressed in red cloth. The Red Maids' School, established in 1634, is now an independent grammar school and the red cloaks are still seen on special occasions.

8

The Chew Valley Area

The River Chew rises near Chewton Mendip in the foothills of the Mendip Hills and, soon after crossing the southern boundary of the County of Avon, it becomes the Chew Valley Lake, a large reservoir which, with others, serves Bristol and its adjoining areas. It flows from the lake again, near Chew Stoke, then through Chew Magna and Compton Dando, to join the Avon at Keynsham, passing through the fertile, undulating country of the Chew Valley during its course. In past times, the River Chew provided power for the numerous mills which stood on its banks, when water was the chief motive power for the local industries.

In this chapter are included neighbouring areas, not in the Chew Valley itself, but either in tributary valleys or on the routes through the valley. One of the main routes from Bristol is the A37, passing, just beyond the south-eastern boundary of the city, through the village of Whitchurch. The old village is almost swallowed up by a large housing estate, while most of the residents work in Bristol. The former civil airfield, opened in 1930 and closed in 1957, in favour of Lulsgate, is quickly becoming covered by factories and stores as part of one of Bristol's adjoining industrial estates. In spite of this development, Whitchurch still remains outside the city boundary, a kind of "buffer state" between the city and the open countryside, and a few yards beyond the traffic signals in the centre of the village, the built-up area immediately ceases and we find ourselves in open country.

Some years ago we were asked to investigate an underground tunnel found at the rear of the Black Lion Inn. I (Edmund) crawled along the tunnel for a short distance to find a dead end and a pit filled with water. I was intrigued by the number of bottle corks floating on the surface and when I looked up, I realized that I was in a well. The tunnel was merely an overflow. I think Whitchurch must have been tunnel-minded at that time, as I was asked to look for another at a farm on the other side of the main road. During dry weather, a light streak was to be seen across the fields. We traced it to a filled-in well, so below ground was probably another overflow. However, as Keynsham Abbey once had a grange and other buildings at Whitchurch and as the well and the farm buildings were ancient, we decided to excavate the well in the hope of medieval material. The team was enthusiastic, until the number of ginger beer bottles, old shoes and an unpleasant smell, led to an unanimous decision to fill it in. Most tunnel investigations prove abortive, but the association of an area with early monastic settlements often gives rise to romantic stories.

In a one-way street adjoining the traffic lights is St Nicholas Church, which has a considerable amount of Norman work, including the tower. There is a story that when Bilbie, the well-known bell founder, was casting a bell for the tower, an elderly lady brought along a great quantity of silver for melting, saying that this way the cleaning would be saved and the silver would always remain in the parish. Unfortunately, St Nicholas is not the only church in the county with the same legend.

Next to the church is the old school, a small pseudo-Gothic building, bearing a partly obliterated plaque, with the words: "School was founded by Miss Sarah Whippie for the instruction of the children of Whitchurch AD 1837." Opposite the old school is a delightful row of cottages and further down the road is Lyons Court, now a farmhouse, but once the home of the Lyons family. The house still retains some of its original medieval work.

Between Whitchurch and the Chew is Queen Charlton, which has all the appearance of a typical old English village. The houses are well spaced round the village green, on which stands the village cross and by the green is the church, while round the corner stands the manor house, still with its mounting block for the carriages. There is one thing out of place and that is the cross, for its original site was on the edge of the village. There it was the centre of the fair which was once held on St Margaret's Day, 20th July, to whom the church is dedicated. W. J. Robinson and Max Barnes tell us of another reason. It seems that boys would play about its steps, no doubt to see who could climb the highest up

Milling flour at Priston Mill

The Packhorse Inn and church, South Stoke

Packhorse bridge and ford, Wellow

Bench poppy-head in St Julian's Church, Wellow

Old Mills Colliery coal tip, Paulton

The Church of the Holy Ghost, Midsomer Norton

Village cross and green, Queen Charlton

Bell ringers at St Margaret's Church, Queen Charlton

Pensford from the old railway viaduct

Old lock-up, Pensford

The ''Druid's Arms'' and cottages, Stanton Drew

Carving of human face on pew in All Saints' Church, Hinton Blewett

Manor house and St Mary's Church, West Harptree

Mill pond, Compton Martin

Rickford village street

Banwell Abbey

the shaft, instead of attending church, but when the cross was sited opposite the church even the most impertinent of boys would feel abashed—or the churchwardens hoped so.

Queen Charlton was once on the highway between Bristol and Bath, since the road along the Avon valley was subject to flood and mud. Queen Elizabeth I came through Queen Charlton *en route* from Bristol to Bath in 1574 and it was she who granted the charter for the St Margaret's Day Fairs. It is not to Elizabeth that the village owes the first part of its name, but probably to Henry VIII's last wife, Catherine Parr, who held Queen Charlton manor with others after the Dissolution. There is some uncertainty about the origin of the name, but we have not found "Queen" in references of 1550 and before. Because of its location on the highway, such as it was, many wealthy people moved from Bristol to Queen Charlton during the last half of the sixteenth century to avoid the plague, but moved back when it had abated.

The manor has an eighteenth-century façade, but some of the interior woodwork, window glass and other features belong to the sixteenth century. On the wall of the hall hangs the head and footboards of a bedstead reputed to have belonged to Catherine Parr. Its carving resembles that of Grinling Gibbons and on the footboard is incised the date 1617. If that is the date of its origin, Catherine Parr would have been dead for quite some time and Grinling Gibbons not yet born, although the carving could, of course, have been done some time after the bedstead was made. One of the rooms is said to have been used by Charles Dickens when on a visit to Queen Charlton. Opposite the house, on the other side of the road, is a small decorated Norman stone arch, leading nowhere. There has been much conjecture about its origin, but Pevsner suggests that it may have been the former doorway of the church. It would seem likely that it had been re-erected here to give an added vista from the house.

The church contains some fine Norman work, but has lost its south transept and the blocked opening is clearly seen inside the church. Two of the columns of the crossing are so close to the blocking wall that one of the curious carved faces on the columns now stares at the wall only a few inches away. These carvings which decorate the columns on each side of the chancel are of human masks on stoat-like bodies. Bizarre creatures seem to be biting the mask facing the wall. Barbara Lowe and Douglas Sprague made a small excavation on the site of the south transept some years ago and found traces of a wall.

Leading from the green is a footpath with a notice: "Priest Path. A medieval footpath leading to Whitchurch", but the last time we were there, we would have had to force our way through the undergrowth. Queen Charlton is what one may call a select village, charming and expensive, with practically no modern development.

A pleasant drive along a narrow country lane, with the scooped-out valley of Wooscombe Bottom on our left and over Fairy Hill, brings us in sight of Compton Dando below on the banks of the Chew, with the church of St Mary the Virgin, a few old houses and a few modern ones. Opposite the inn, "The Gamekeeper", is the small village school and a short lane leads to the church with its Perpendicular tower and part of a Roman altar inserted into the foot of the north-east buttress of the chancel. The stone is believed to have been found during excavations at the Roman baths at Bath. It is badly worn, but is carved with the figures of Roman gods. The church was restored during the eighteenth century and again in Victorian times.

Near Compton Dando and also on the Chew is Woollard. It had a medieval bridge, one of several over the Chew, but like bridges at Keynsham and Pensford, it was washed away by the great flood in 1968 and has been replaced by a wide modern bridge. All that is left of the old bridge are a few stones adjoining the new bridge. There is a memorial plaque erected to mark the Jubilee in 1977 which states, "These stones formed part of the base of the old Woollard bridge which was destroyed by flood July 10th 1968." The Bell Farm, which in summer sells lemonade, sweets and cigarettes, was once the Bell Inn and on its flank wall can be seen a blocked pre-Reformation window. The building has a very nice hooded doorway. A pretty row of former labourers' cottages is called Paradise Row, dated 1782, and has been converted into very pleasant dwellings. In the past, Woollard made full use of its Chew water power for driving a grist mill, which in the 1730s became a tin-plate rolling mill. It was taken over about 1781 by Elton and Tyndall, copper manufacturers, and by 1796 had been acquired by the John Freeman and Copper Company who already held several other mills on the same river. The mills closed down in the mid nineteenth century. Like many mills, the Woollard mill is now a private house.

Contemporary with the metal mills, another industry was tanning, for the Brodribbs were tanners here from 1745. A member of this large family, who followed a very different career was Henry Brodribb, better known as Sir Henry Irving, the actor. Like the metal work, tanning is no longer carried on at Woollard and the water power of the Chew no longer drives the mills.

A short distance up the river is Publow, where the John Freeman and Copper Company had another mill, which closed in 1860. Like many other villages which once had flourishing industries, you would not think that this small quiet place ever resounded to the noise of a mill. The Chew Valley was in Somerset before the local government reorganization of 1974 and the central feature of Publow is its fine Somerset church tower. The church, dedicated to All Saints, was one of those held by Keynsham Abbey until the Dissolution and near the church the road crosses over a small medieval bridge, to reach the larger village of Pensford.

Pensford is on the busy road from Bristol to Wells and is overlooked by the massive railway viaduct which was built in 1873 but has not carried a train for some years. The Bristol to Frome line carried its last passenger in 1959 and finally closed as a goods line after the 1968 flood. The metals have been taken up and the local people now take their dogs for a walk along the old track. From the viaduct there is a marvellous bird's-eye view of Pensford below and across the fields, the great church tower of little Publow rises above the surrounding trees as if from a small oasis. At the road end of the viaduct, an open space that was once the station yard still has a few coal bunkers and an old railway shed is now used as a garage, while the adjoining platforms are growing a covering of grass.

The old road through Pensford crossed the Chew by the ancient Chew Bridge which withstood the Chew floods of 1968, although the bridge on the main road was washed away. Until a new bridge could be erected, the medieval Chew Bridge had to take the main road traffic and so, for a time, part of the old route once more came into use. The modern road cuts Pensford in half, for the old road continues on the other side of the main road and turns at the little green opposite the octagonal eighteenth-century lock-up, (where unruly drunks and criminals were locked up for the night) past the "George and Dragon", an old coaching inn of 1752, to join the main road again near the disused Pensford colliery. The village was built along its old road on both sides of the main road. By the medieval bridge, three buildings are linked together to form the interesting Bridge House. The eighteenth-century part arched over the mill stream, an offshoot of the

Chew, is known as the Weaver's Cottage and the corner building is an attractive sixteenth-century timber-framed house with an overhanging upper storey and gable with a fine many-paned Georgian window of the shop type on the ground floor. Inside Bridge House in a hooded alcove is a coat of arms which may have been removed from elsewhere. It has been repainted and the original colours are not known, but the coat of arms may have been that of the Rodney family.

Over the old bridge is the church of St Thomas à Becket, unused as a church since the flood damage of 1968, although the clock still chimes out the hours and the weathercock still stands proudly above the tower, despite having lost its compass arms. The church is now the Becket Centre where local people hold exhibitions, meetings and other events, still serving the community in a secular manner. The churchgoers of Pensford now attend the church at Publow. The flood damage to the church brought matters to a head, but even before the damage, these two churches so near each other, with the cost of heating and repairs, were too large for the dwindling congregations. If you go up the turning adjoining the "Rising Sun" public house to the car park, you pass some eighteenth-century buildings, one bearing the date between its upper windows of 1734. From the car park, a path leads by a footbridge over the old mill pond, but the mill has long since disappeared, although its wheel pit and ground-level features are still apparent.

Like several Avon villages, where water power was available for the fulling mills, Pensford became a cloth centre. Weavers set up their looms in these villages to avoid the restrictions of the city guilds. The trade was flourishing in Pensford by the fourteenth century and Leland in the sixteenth century described it as a "market townlet occupied with clothinge". The industry was still in existence at the beginning of the eighteenth century, but shared the decline of the West country's woollen trade due to competition from the north and economic factors.

Coal mining subsequently became its chief industry, but that in its turn disappeared in 1958 with the closure of the Pensford colliery. A reminder of the mining days is the Miners' Institute near the Red Lion Inn. A retired miner, Harry Dodds, who came from Newcastle forty-five years ago to seek work at the Pensford colliery, told us that the coal outcrops nearly to the surface at the foot of the viaduct. There is still some evidence of the local village trades. Part of Bridge House was a saddler's shop and a wooden rack of hooks used by the saddler still remains behind the front door. We asked Harry Dodds what the single-storey building was by Bridge House and which still had the remains of a forge. He replied, "Oh, that was where they used to put the iron tyres on the wooden wheels, but it is now used by a builder who is also the undertaker." This reminded us of a number of villages we once knew where the local undertaker was also the village carpenter, the estate agent and furniture remover and perhaps even the coal merchant. The growth of the village can still be traced in the architectural style of the buildings, the oldest cottages round the church and the Chew, the eighteenth-century houses climbing the hill along the old road, the nineteenth-century miners' housing and further on the outskirts, modern development.

On the house on the corner of the main road and Church Street, opposite the war memorial, a marker indicates the flood level on 10th July 1968 and there is another marker on the same side of Church Street, nearer its other junction with the main road. It is surprising how the older buildings stood up to the force of water, which, in some cases, reached the bedroom windows and not only in the 1968 flood, but the flood of 1888 when the Chew overflowed its banks and the water rose to four feet within the church.

Today, although some residents are engaged in agriculture and local trades, Pensford is a village with a strong commuter element. Apart from the modern development, several old houses have been restored and converted for modern use, but externally they still retain their character, for their owners take a great pride in their ancient features. In one case, the whole of the roof was stripped and lined, but the old tiles, characteristic of Pensford, were replaced.

North-west of Pensford is Norton Malreward, a small village in a picturesque setting, overlooked by the hill and Iron Age earthworks of Maes Knoll. The name "Malreward" has more than one interpretation and the most romantic concerns Sir John Hautville, a man of great strength who lived in Norton Hautville now Norton Hawkfield. Legend says that Edward I heard of the feats of this giant of a man and during a visit to the neighbourhood, asked Sir John to give a demonstration of his strength. Sir John seized three of the King's heaviest soldiers and with one under each arm and with one in his teeth, he climbed the steps of the tower of the parish church to the top. On the way, the soldiers under his arms started to struggle, so he killed them by crushing them with his arms. The King was so impressed that he gave him land in the parish. Sir John Hautville thought this was a bad or "mal" reward for his efforts. He was so disgusted that he went to the top of Maes Knoll and hurled a huge stone from the top. It landed in a field and is known today as Hautville's Quoit, although there seems little doubt that it forms part of the much older complex of the Stanton Drew stone circles. Sir John is said to have been buried in a church at Norton Hautville and when it was demolished, his wooden effigy was transferred to the church at Chew Magna. Another suggestion is that the name "Malreward" came from a family of that name, a more prosaic explanation, but more likely. The church tower at Norton Malreward which Sir John Hautville is reputed to have climbed with his burden is thirteenth century, but most of the church was rebuilt in 1861. It contains a fine, but restored, late Norman chancel arch. The porch holds an interesting collection of grave-stones, including the one of Mary Sheappard, inserted in the wall, with this inscription, "This tender one beneath this stone did hourt to none". Above it on the wall is an ancient coat of arms. The approach to the church is by a short earthen track overhung by a damson tree and in the churchyard is a very large ancient yew. From the churchyard is a good view of the adjoining early Georgian manor house, now Manor Farm, with its Ionic and Tuscan pilasters. Half a mile north of the village, are the last visible signs westward of the Wansdyke which climbs to Maes Knoll.

A short distance along the road from Norton Malreward is Stanton Drew. The first building the traveller sees before turning down into the village is the quaint white and thatched fifteenth-century hexagonal house, which became a toll-house in the eighteenth century, a reminder of the days of the turnpike trusts. Between the toll-house and the village is the fifteenth-century stone bridge crossing the Chew. It is a picturesque and quiet village, well away from the noise of the main roads. There are some small modern houses but these are inconspicuous among the stone-built seventeenth- and eighteenth-century houses of the village. Its name "Stanton" means "stone town", but whether this refers to the building stone of the houses or the famous stone circles is not known. The other part of its name "Drew" is a family name, of the Drew or Drogo family who once held land here. Among its stone buildings is the old rectory, known as the Rectory Farm House, with fine mullioned windows and, on the opposite side of the road, is the Court, a mid eighteenth-century building which was once the Manor House. Nearby is a house with a bull-nose end abutting on to the road. Like other old buildings of Stanton Drew, this is a protected building. To the east of the church, Church Farm has some fourteenth-century features and is interesting enough to be visited by architectural students. The church of St Mary did not escape the extensive restoration of many of our churches during the nineteenth century, although parts may be dated to the thirteenth century.

The local inn is the "Druid's Arms", with its inn sign of a venerable Druid. It is so named because it was once believed that the stone circles, not far from the church, were connected with the ancient Celtic priesthood, a belief that was mainly due to the fertile imagination of the eighteenth-century antiquarian the eccentric William Stukeley, who made an intensive study of Avebury and Stonehenge. As the Druids did not appear until about eighteen centuries after the stones were erected, the circles were already ancient and no doubt ruinous in their time. and there is no evidence that the Druids ever used them. It is highly probable that the circles were temples of some kind, but we know nothing of the religious life of the Bronze Age people who erected them. Like all stone circles, the Stanton Drew circles have their legends. The best known one is about a wedding party, who were dancing on a Saturday. At midnight the piper refused to play on into the Sabbath. The irate bride said she would get one from hell if necessary, but the situation was saved by a kindly piper who turned up and offered to play. Once they had started to dance, the music grew faster and faster and the dancers were unable to stop, realizing too late that the new piper was the Devil himself. When the music ceased, they were turned to stone and so the stones today are sometimes called the "weddings".

Less than two miles westward, along the B3130, is Chew Magna, so called because it was probably the most important place on the river. It certainly today has an air of importance with its long main street with old houses built above raised pavements and colourful inn signs. Stream and river make it an island village connected by the Chew bridges. Leland, in the sixteenth century, called it "a pretty clothing town" and its past prosperity is reflected in its fine buildings. It is now mainly a commuter village, but is still a centre for much of the Chew Valley and because it is a conservation area, there is but sparse modern development.

The central part of the village is dominated by the great fifteenth-century tower, almost one hundred feet high, of St Andrew's Church. There are still traces of a Norman church round the south door and the rest of the church contains Early English and Perpendicular work. In a cusped recess is a wooden effigy reputed to be that of Sir John Hautville, renowned for his feats of strength at Norton Malreward and Maes Knoll. It is one of those rare wooden effigies and shows the knight cross-legged and leaning on one elbow. It is supposed to have come from the demolished chapel at Norton Hawkfield, but there is some doubt whether the effigy is really that of Sir John. The north chapel contains the fifteenth-century effigies of Sir John Loe and his lady. The armoured figure of Sir John is 7 feet, 4 inches long and his feet rest on a lion, while those of his lady rest on a dog. Another interesting memorial is that of Edward Baber who died in 1578 and his wife who died in 1601. They wear double ruffs round their necks and their hands are raised in prayer. He is dressed as a sergeant at arms, while she wears a black gown and a Paris head-dress.

Adjoining the churchyard and separated from it by a high wall is Chew Court, once a palace of the Bishop of Bath and Wells. At one time, the Bishop held considerable land in the area, hence the place names, Bishops Chew, one of the old names for Chew Magna, and Bishop Sutton. Perhaps the most conspicuous building in the village adjoins the churchyard gate. It is early sixteenth century with an ornate façade in marked contrast to the modern bank premises next door and overlooks the small triangular green which is the hub of the village. It is known as the Old Schoolroom, but was originally the church ales house, where the churchwardens brewed the church ales on festive occasions. An external side staircase leads to a hall with a fine timbered roof and the ground floor has a large fire opening extending the whole width of the great room. The facing surround has long since gone and the opening is now partly concealed by a cupboard conversion. Here the churchwardens brewed the church ales. The building is leased from the diocesan authorities and used by the Chew Valley Youth Services Committee as a youth centre, intended for the whole of the Chew Valley, although local youth centres have now been established in some villages.

Just within the churchyard gate, next to the old church ales house, is the upturned base of an ancient cross known as a "resting stone" on which the coffin used to be placed before its final journey to the church. Across the road are two fine old public houses, the plaster-faced "Pelican" and the stone-faced "Bear and Swan" and between them is the Old Bakehouse with its added bay shop window. Although the "Bear and Swan" shows the date 1886 this is a restoration date and not that of the original building. It was certainly there in 1776 according to deeds of sale and was probably built earlier in that century.

Only a mile south-west of Chew Magna is Chew Stoke, just west of the river from which it derives part of its name. There is quite a lot of new development, but the centre of the old village is hidden away off the main road and is still untouched. A stream flowing through the village, on its way to join the Chew, forms a low cascade under a narrow bridge, which leads to a street lined with eighteenth-century houses, newly restored.

The Old Rectory, on the way to the church, was believed to have been built by the rector, Sir John Barry, in 1529, although it has had many alterations since that time. The south front of the house is ornate with carvings of shields bearing the arms of the St Loe family, who were once the chief landowners in this area. The churchyard gate bears a lamp which was provided by public subscription to commemorate Queen Victoria's Jubilee of 1897. There are two objects salvaged from the floods when the Chew Valley Reservoir was constructed in the 1950s. One, near the churchyard wall, is the base and stump of a shaft of an ancient cross and nearby is a plaque which states that it was removed from the hamlet of Moreton during the construction of the Chew Valley Lake and restored by Bristol Waterworks Company. The other, within the porch on the left of the church door, is a stone figure holding an anchor. This came from Walley Court, demolished in 1951 to make way for the reservoir, although it may have formed part of a chimney piece from an earlier building on the same site. The story goes that it was presented to a member of the Gilbert family, then living at the Court, by Queen Elizabeth I, but the story is unconfirmed. The church, dedicated to St Andrew, has an impressive tower, with a very tall stair turret spirelet. Most of the interior is Victorian restoration overlying the original fifteenth-century work and there is a multitude of Victorian angels adding to the decoration. Another item which catches the eye is the enormous quartz crystal jammed into the foot of the eagle-shaped lectern.

A famous family of Chew Stoke, known not for their pedigree but for their skill, was that of the Bilbies, who were responsible in the eighteenth century for the casting of church bells. Many of these still exist in church towers over a wide area. So proud were they of their work, that they hardly ever failed to advertise their skill on their products, sometimes making quite pithy inscriptions, such as at Mark in Somerset:

Come Here Brother Founders Here You may See
What Sort of a Workman Young Bilbie may be.

One story about the family is that the wife of Francis Popham of Marksbury visited the Bilbies when a bell was being cast and threw in a large quantity of silver to sweeten the sound of the bell, a variation of the story as is told about the casting of the bell at Whitchurch.

Between Chew Stoke and Bishop Sutton is the great reservoir, Chew Valley Lake, with ten miles of shore, officially opened in 1956 as one of the main sources of Bristol's water supply. With Blagdon Lake, another large reservoir nearby, it forms Avon's "Lake District" and attracts many tourists to the area, not only those who come to admire the marvellous views of the lakes, but fishermen and sailing enthusiasts. Then, too, birdwatchers come to study the great variety of bird life which is to be found on the waters. As motorists we find that in the high season we are condemned to follow slow coaches, bearing sightseers along narrow lanes giving views of the lakes. The long street of Chew Magna, on one of the main routes to the lakes, suffers some congestion, but the village centre of Chew Stoke, just off the route, is as quiet as it always was.

On the other side of the Chew Valley Lake is Bishop Sutton, which once possessed a coal mine and provided coal for the resmelting of the lead debris left behind by the old miners on Mendip. The mine closed early in this century. Today it is a straggling commuter village for Bristol and Bath, with many modern houses and bungalows and a church built in its mining days, in the nineteenth century.

Just outside Bishop Sutton is Sutton Court, hidden away in its own grounds out of view. William de Sutton built a fortified house about 1310, but only a wall and a square tower with the lower stages of its stair turret, remain of the original building. The Court eventually passed to the St Loes and Sir William St Loe married Elizabeth Hardwick in the sixteenth century, when major additions were made to the house. She was better known as "Bess of Hardwick" because of Hardwick Hall which she later built. Bess had been married twice already, outlived Sir William and married yet a further husband whom she survived. Having outlived all her husbands and in so doing amassed a fortune, she lived into her nineties. She settled Sutton Court on her son Charles Cavendish by her second husband, but later the property passed to the Strachey family. Sir Edward Strachey who succeeded to the Court in 1858, engaged Wyatt to remodel the house, although its outer form seems to have changed but little.

A little south of Sutton Court is Stowey, hardly big enough for a hamlet, yet possessing a church. It is approached by a hilly road with a string of stone cottages and its two important buildings, Stowey House and the church, stand next to each other. Stowey House is a farm, standing well back from the road. No high walls surround it, so we have an uninterrupted view of the castellated house. The original gabled part of Stowey House is seventeenth century, but was considerably extended in Georgian times.

The small church dedicated to St Nicholas and St Mary is small and reputed to date from the thirteenth century. Inside it has a wagon ceiling and the walls are painted with religious scenes, the work of Henry Strachey in 1915. The only industry to be seen at Stowey today is agriculture, but once a mill crushed ochre here, used for making pigment for marking sheep, but it was apparently eclipsed by ochre works at Winford and the substitution of crushed berries from Brazil. Another lost industry was a glass works at Sutton Wick. Now the combined areas of Stowey and Bishop Sutton are known as Stowey Sutton.

To the south of Bishop Sutton is Hinton Blewett, approached like a number of villages in this district by undulating winding lanes. It is a picturesque village, where church, pub and some old houses overlook a pleasant village green, known as the "Barbury". On one of our visits, a rally of veteran cars slowly paraded past the green and added to the general atmosphere of bygone days. Known in the Domesday Book as Hantone, it did not acquire the name of Blewett until after the Bluet family came to live there in the fourteenth century. The church is of mixed architectural styles, with the chancel arch thirteenth century, the chancel and north aisle sixteenth century and the tower rebuilt in the early eighteenth century. The five bells were cast in 1708 by the Bilbies of Chew Stoke and just to remind you, the tenor bell bears the inscription "Bilbie cast all wee 1708". The pulpit, converted from a three decker, is dated 1638 and the font is Norman. In 1928, the woodwork of the pews was rearranged and one of the pieces, with a human face carved by a medieval craftsman, is to be seen on the front of the pews.

A well-established family in the seventeenth century were the Thierys who were refugees from religious persecution in France. Religious persecution nearly ruined the church in the eighteenth century, when the minister John Brookes chose a Roman Catholic wife, just at the time when feeling against the proposal to restore legal rights to Roman Catholics was aroused. An irate mob set out from Bath to burn the church, but were intercepted *en route* by the army.

From Prospect Stile on high ground just west of Hinton Blewett can be seen one of the finest panoramic views of the Chew Valley Lake and the hills beyond, Although the village is still largely unspoilt, the attractions of the "Lake District" has brought an increasing amount of traffic to this quiet place.

A really amazing survival from the past is the church of St James at Cameley, between Hinton Blewett and Temple Cloud, which Sir John Betjeman described as a "Rip-Van-Winkle's" church, looking as if it had been asleep for a century and a half. In fact, the last improvement was a gallery, erected in 1819, along one side of the church, as an extension of the 1711 gallery across the end of the nave and reached by an exterior flight of stone steps. Even the Royal Coat of Arms hanging on the gallery is that of Charles I, which is in itself a rarity. As is not unusual, the oldest item in the church is the Norman font, while the Jacobean pulpit, with its sounding board and its several box pews and rough benching are reminiscent of one of those old prints showing the pastor ranting forth with flying arms to a half-sleeping congregation.

The church has the largest assembly of ancient wall paintings that we have seen for such a small building. On one of the chancel arch supports are the three leopards of England, those of Edward I and on the other support, the chevrons of Eleanor of Castille, his queen. On the south wall of the nave are painted the arms of James I, which include the Scottish thistle. Near the chancel arch are the arms of Charles I. These are but a few of the designs in the church, but the earliest is probably the imitation stone walling painted on the north wall, attributed to the eleventh century. The others are of various dates, such as the jester of the fourteenth century behind the elaborately carved box pew known as Samuel

Oliver's pew in the north-east corner of the nave. In front of Samuel Oliver's pew is a very narrow pew leading up to the pulpit which was erected by John Wilcox in 1637. This was where the minister would sit before taking his place in the pulpit and was used as a reader's desk. High box pews occupy the south-east corner of the nave and adjoin the south doorway.

In the eighteenth century, most of the villagers moved to the hamlet of Temple Cloud, a mile to the east, to take advantage of the better communications provided by the turnpike road, so that Temple Cloud became the village and Cameley the hamlet. St Barnabas Church was built at Temple Cloud in 1925 and both churches continued in use until 1956 when St James at Cameley was closed because of the poor state of repair. However, with voluntary help, the church was put into order and reopened in 1960, but finally on the first day of 1980, it ceased to be the parish church, although occasional services are still held there.

The origin of the name of Temple Cloud is intriguing, but several obscure suggestions about it have been put forward, including associations with Knight Templars and Roman temples. Unlike Cameley, it became a thriving industrial centre in the nineteenth century with haematite mines, quarries, brick-works and collieries, but these have long since closed down and, for many people, today, Temple Cloud is no more than a familiar name on the A37 road from Bristol to Wells and Shepton Mallet.

9

Under Mendip

Avon's southern boundary runs through the foothills which form the northern fringe of Mendip, a range of hills orientated east to west and terminating as Brean Down at Weston-super-Mare, to reappear in the Bristol Channel as the small rocky islands of Flat and Steep Holm. The hills themselves are a conspicuous feature seen from the main roads which radiate south and south-west from Bristol to Wells, Bridgwater and Weston-super-Mare. The villages of the foothills are set in fertile undulating country, very different from the plateau upland of Mendip in the neighbouring county of Somerset.

Less than two miles south of Temple Cloud on the A37 road from Bristol to Wells and Shepton Mallet is Farrington Gurney, right on the boundary of Avon and Somerset. In the Domesday Book it is known as Ferentone, while the second part of its name comes from the Gournay family, once lords of the manor. Thomas de Gournay was involved in the murder of Edward II at Berkeley Castle, not far from Avon's northern boundary. When Edward III was seeking vengeance for his father's death, Thomas fled to Spain. He was arrested there and was executed on the way back to England for trial. As at Englishcombe, his estates at Farrington Gurney were seized by the Crown and eventually became part of the Duchy of Cornwall's possessions. A branch of the family returned to Farrington Gurney, but not to their vast estates, for three hundred years later, Mr Richard Mogg, whose ancestral tree included the de Gournays, built himself a manor house there early in the seventeenth century, a fine gabled building, now known as Little Manor. The old parsonage is another interesting building which was built about 1700 and is near the junction of the Radstock and the A37 Shepton Mallet roads. Some way out to the east of the village, set in the midst of a field, is the pseudo-Norman church of St John the Baptist which replaced an older church demolished in 1843.

Farrington Gurney had its share of the mining activities of the Somerset Coal Field and there was a colliery there in the 1700s. Coal production in the coal field declined in the 1920s and there was consequently much unemployment but in 1924, about fifty unemployed miners contributed five pounds each and obtained a licence to start a drift mine near Farrington Gurney at Marsh Lane and the Government allowed them to continue to draw unemployment pay during the time they developed the working. Eventually it produced over a hundred tons a week, but was closed by the National Coal Board in 1949 as uneconomic.

To the west of Farrington Gurney is East Harptree, a straggling village on the northern slopes of the Mendip Hills. A conspicuous landmark from afar is the chimney of the old lead resmelting works on Smitham Hill above the village. Once there were several of these chimneys on Mendip, but they have disappeared one by one and only this one remains, restored and preserved. The works were not used for the mining of lead ore, but for resmelting the debris left behind by the "old men", the old miners.

The church of St Lawrence has an enormous monument to Sir John Newton and his twelve daughters and eight sons. The monument once stood in the chancel, but was moved to a more convenient position in the wide porch. Sir John died in 1568. Some little distance to the south-west of the church is the site of Richmont Castle, once the stronghold of the de Gournays, but now almost obliterated. Much of its demolition was done by Sir John, who used the building as a convenient stone quarry. The village itself, with its grey stone houses and cottages climbing the Mendip slopes and the picturesque inn and farm each side of the church, is quite unspoilt and is a conservation area.

West Harptree is about a mile to the west and a mile south of Chew Valley Lake. It is at the meeting of several roads and its position means that there is a lot of traffic, particularly in summer when visitors tour round the lakes. At the road junction is the church of St Mary, rebuilt in 1865, but retaining its Norman tower, although with an added spire. Like many houses in its vicinity, the building is of dolomitic conglomerate, one of the several rocks which form the Mendip Hills. Opposite the church is the early seventeenth-century gabled Gournay Court, an impressive house in which older work is incorporated. Next to the church is another ancient house, the Tilley Manor House built in 1659, although its façade was altered in the eighteenth century. It is decorated with stone carved coats of arms over each of its four ground-floor windows and over the entrance. This fine building is now the farmhouse to the adjoining farm. There were apparently two manors at West Harptree, one held for a time by the Gournays, whose manor house probably stood on the site of Gournay Court, and the Tilley Manor, once held by the Tilley or Tilly family until it passed out of their hands in Edward IV's reign.

The junction of the roads at West Harptree forms a triangle which is the centre of the village. Here there is a small flower bed known as Jubilee Garden, planted to commemorate Elizabeth II's Jubilee, a contribution from the villagers. The Triangle, overlooked by the church, by Parsonage Farm, a yellow stuccoed house believed to be the oldest building in the village and by the old village school, was once the village pond. Across the road is the Crown Inn which replaced a thatched house. The National school, built in 1852, closed during the 1970s and is a good example of the way in which many of these Victorian school buildings are converted to modern use. The schoolhouse was sold as a private residence and the schoolroom itself was converted into a house by inserting a floor to form another storey and providing dormer windows at roof level to match the remainder of the building. The typical Victorian schoolroom had a very lofty ceiling to provide a healthy amount of fresh air and tall windows to give plenty of light, but high enough to stop pupils gazing out of them. This type of conversion turns these buildings into very pleasant dwellings and so preserves the outward form of what was an important part of village life.

The village once had an eighteenth-century corn mill down by the River Chew, known as the Stratford Mill. Although out of action for many years, it was used during the 1939-45 war for grinding corn when more local land was brought under the plough to augment the national food reserves. Stratford Mill was on land needed for the Chew Valley reservoir and would have been destroyed, but happily it was removed and rebuilt with the original machinery on the Hazel Brook in Blaise Castle grounds on the north-western outskirts of Bristol.

Compton Martin, about a mile west of West Harptree, is a village very much on a main road, for the A368, which runs under the northern slopes of Mendip from Weston-super-Mare to West Harptree, is a busy route. In spite of the traffic, the mill pond, the hillside church and the old cottages and farmhouses, all help the village to keep its rural atmosphere. The pond is fed by the River Yeo, a major contributor to the Yeo Reservoir or Blagdon Lake and which finally, as a sluggish stream, flows into the Bristol Channel at Woodspring Bay. Because they are in the water catchment area, Compton Martin, Blagdon, Butcombe and some outlying farms are provided with a sewerage system and sewage disposal plant to prevent the possibility of contamination.

Much of the Norman work in our churches has suffered because of rebuilding, but at St Michael's Church, Compton Martin, the fine Norman architecture was saved by an accident during an extensive rebuilding in the later fourteenth century. Apparently, as the masons began work on the chancel arch, the building began to sink and the results of this settlement are clearly visible today. Apart from the tower and some additions, the builders seem to have left much of the Norman work alone. One fascinating feature of the church is the diagonal fluting cut into one of the Norman columns, giving it a twisted appearance, similar to columns in Durham Cathedral. The column was plastered over and it was only during the nineteenth century when the plaster was removed during restoration work, that the fluting was revealed.

The church has a delightful little chancel, with a ceiling divided by two diagonal ribs and is separated from the rest of the church by a Norman arch. Here can be seen the work of the rebuilders in the peculiarly flattened arch and a column leaning outwards, the result of the settlement, and in the conversion of the first south arch of the Norman arcading to the Perpendicular style. A new south aisle was added, higher than the original one and because of this, the once external clerestory wall with the old window openings is now within the church. The holes which once took the aisle roof rafters are below the clerestory openings and the present aisle rafters rest on what was once the Norman external corbels carved with heads, typical of Norman work. Comparison with the north exterior nave wall makes the architectural history clear, providing a good example of how the masons of the Perpendicular style started their conversions.

In a recess on floor level in the north aisle, is a painted stone effigy of a civilian in a red robe, believed to be that of Thomas Moreton. His family gave its name to a village now under the waters of the Chew Valley Lake. Moat Farm is an interesting moated house a mile north of the village and is reputed to contain stonework of the former Bickfield Nunnery. It is said that the splendid screen of the south chantry chapel came from this nunnery.

Like many villages built near streams and rivers, Compton Martin had its mill and the village pond was originally the mill pond, the water being artificially held back and in places at a higher level than the adjoining land. On our last visit in 1980, the old mill house was still standing and was being converted to a dwelling-house using certain of the old walls and rebuilding the remainder with original stones and using the old roof cladding. The slot for the water wheel is still visible, while the mill stone lies in the yard of Dukes Farm next to the pond. Close by was the sheep wash site where farmers used to dip their sheep brought down from Mendip. It is now paved over and provided with seats and tables for the public in commemoration of the Jubilee of Elizabeth II.

Around Compton Martin and other villages on the edge of Mendip were once local industries, which have long since disappeared, connected with the woollen and cloth trade, such as the growing of teasels for dressing the cloth and of woad for dyeing and, not far away, the digging of fuller's earth for the fulling mills.

Compton Martin was the birthplace of St Wulfric of Haselbury, who died in his cell at Haselbury Plucknett, near Crewkerne, in 1154. He was reputed to have had the power of seeing into the future and foretold the accession to the throne of King Stephen.

The road westward from Compton Martin passes beneath the steep, heavily wooded Mendip slopes and, in less than two miles, a minor road leads straight into the village of Ubley, a peaceful backwater although just off the busy main road. Quiet and secluded, with its village green with a restored medieval cross, bordered by an ancient church and pleasant houses, it has the look of a village the world has passed by. Yet, it has an industry apart from agriculture and saw mills, an industry famous the world over. Conveniently situated between the two lakes, those of Chew and Blagdon, is a trout hatchery, where brown and rainbow trout are hatched and the eggs sent over long distances, so that fish from Ubley hatcheries are to be found, not only in the local lakes, but in rivers in Africa, South America, New Zealand, the Far East and many other places. A number of people living at Ubley, therefore, have no need to commute to the cities for work, as agriculture, the hatcheries, the saw mills and even the reservoirs themselves, provide local occupations. On the edge of the village some modern houses have been built for those who have settled there to enjoy the village and the local scenery or to work in the area.

The thirteenth-century church, with the chained copy of the Paraphrase of the Gospels by Erasmus of 1552, its Jacobean wooden pulpit and parish chest, is dedicated to St Bartholomew on whose feast day was held the annual fair. The right to hold the fair and to hold the weekly market on Mondays was granted in Edward II's reign. As in the case of many villages, improved communication to more convenient centres has caused the market to disappear a long time ago, as did the mansion which stood in Ubley in Henry VI's time, with its 140-acre deer park. Church towers, not spires, are usual in most of the county, but a spire has been added to the tower of St Bartholomew's Church. Although the church is mainly of the thirteenth century, the aisles were added in the fifteenth century, not uncommon additions at this time. There are no pews. The congregation sit on ordinary chairs and these are only in the nave.

One of the best-known villages in the area is Blagdon because it gives its name to the Yeo Reservoir, better known as Blagdon Lake, which, with the Chew Valley Reservoir, forms Avon's miniature lake district. Blagdon is by far the older of the two reservoirs. It was begun in 1889 and completed in 1901 and its construction, unlike that of the Chew Reservoir, did not involve the destruction of villages or buildings.

Blagdon stands on the slopes of the Mendips above the lake, crowned by its church, whose great fifteenth-century Somerset tower of 116 feet is a landmark for miles around. Except for the tower, it was rebuilt in 1909 by Lord Winterstoke, replacing another church built in 1822. Lord Winterstoke belonged to the Wills family of tobacco fame who did much to preserve and enhance the attractions of the village. The only relic of the Norman church which stood on the site is the stone piscina in the south wall of the chancel. From 1762-4, the Reverend Augustus Toplady, who wrote the well-known hymn "Rock of Ages", was the curate of Blagdon and a letter written by him hangs framed near the vestry.

Near the church is the New Inn, in spite of its name the oldest inn in Blagdon, a sixteenth-century house, once a cider house. From the inn and the church, Church Street ascends the hill to the main road and on the left is Hannah More House, once a school set up by Hannah More, who did so much for the education of poor country children at the end of the eighteenth century. Near the main road is the village school, with its conspicuous belfry, built in 1842.

A footpath from the churchyard leads down to Timswell, where up into the 1920s villagers used to come with yoke and buckets to collect their water supply. It was cleaned and restored as a project for Elizabeth II's Jubilee. The other well was Lower Well down the hill below the New Inn, where a spring issues from the stone walling. From Timswell, a footpath continues up the sloping open land by the playing-fields to the western part of Blagdon, the main part of the village. Here are the village shops and the village club provided for the inhabitants by the Wills family. Here, too, are some ancient houses such as Court Farm and Blagdon House and Bell Square, with the old Bell Inn and cottages much altered, but probably built in Tudor times.

Blagdon, with its old houses, cottages and inns, particularly the charming cluster round the church, is a conservation area. Modern development is chiefly restricted to an area to the north of the main road, where some local authority housing, elderly people's bungalows and some private modern houses exist. Because of its lovely setting and the unspoilt character of the village, cottages and houses are quickly snapped up and reno-vated by comfortably off commuters and retired people, known, we are told, by some villagers as the "cottage gentry". However, village life is extremely well integrated and there is no friction between the newcomers and the well-rooted inhabitants. There is a real feeling for the village and a good deal of voluntary work is done to improve the amenities, whether it be restoring Timswell or initiating a private bus service to help those without cars.

About a mile west of Blagdon is Rickford, a pleasant little hamlet. It had a chapel once, but that is now a masonic hall, and Burrington church is not far away. It also had a mill pond, now a pleasant pool, complete with cascade and from it the water flows down one side of the road and then the other, crossed by small bridges to adjoining bungalows. In summer there are usually two or three small children paddling and fishing for tadpoles and minnows. It is a one-road hamlet and near the ford at one end is the Mendip Painting Centre, once a carpenter's workshop. Now painting classes are held there under expert tuition. Most of Rickford belongs to the Wills estate and is controlled by the Langford Court Estate office. The estate owners have kept a careful control in preserving much of its original character. Even the waterworks building matches the former chapel, while the brewers have managed to retain the rural atmosphere of their public house the "Plume of Feathers".

There are no shops in Rickford, neither at first sight is there any industry, but an opening by the "Plume of Feathers" leads into a factory courtyard. The manufacturers are cabinet-makers in various kinds of work, but chiefly specialize in scientific instrument box making. The older part of the building was built about 1882 and was used as a printing works. During the 1914-18 war it became an army shirt factory and Mr Peter Heimann, the managing director of the present cabinet-making firm, told us that when they removed some floor boards, they found hundreds of shirt buttons and printer's type.

The mill, of which only the mill pond remains, once straddled the stream and was used during the first half of the nineteenth century by the Hall family of paper makers. There were several paper mills in the area during this time, an industry which may have originated partly through the Huguenot refugee paper makers in the area. Today much of Rickford water is piped to Blagdon Lake.

Burrington is known because of its famous combe, but the village lies in an adjoining valley centred round a large triangle formed by the junction of a side road. Along this side road most of the development in modern times has taken place. Facing the triangle is the school and the church of Holy Trinity, a late Perpendicular building, containing fragments of fifteenth-century glass over the north door.

Burrington, like Blagdon and Langford, once had a railway station, but the line closed for passenger traffic in 1931. As the road through Burrington leads only to footpaths, very few of the thousands attracted to Burrington Combe visit the village. Tourists come to the Combe, not only for its scenery, but to see the great cleft, where the Reverend Augustus Toplady, one-time curate at Blagdon, sheltered from a storm and subsequently wrote the famous hymn "Rock of Ages". Most weekends, summer or winter, there are helmeted and boiler-suit clad cavers in the Combe, entering or emerging from such caves as Goat-

church and Sidcot Hole, while the large rock opening almost
opposite the Rock of Ages is Aveline's Hole which once produced
human skeletons and other relics of the Old Stone Age.

A mile from Burrington is Langford. There is an Upper and
Lower Langford, but the village is at Lower Langford. Just before
entering it from Burrington, we pass Langford Court, the home
of Sir John Wills. Although of Elizabethan origin, it was much
altered in the eighteenth century by Dr T. S. Whalley, a young
clergyman who married the heiress, an immensely rich widow.
He liked living in style and got through a considerable proportion
of his wife's fortune in ten years. After his wife's death, he
married another heiress and this time it took him eight years to
squander her fortune. A widower again, he found another rich
widow, or so he thought, and they married in the belief that each
was wealthy. By the time he had to give her a house in Bath and
make a settlement on her, he was a broken man both in health
and finance. At 82 years of age, he went to France and it is said he
died there in a common lodging-house.

Another large house in Langford is Langford House, now used
by Bristol University as a School of Veterinary Science. A number
of new buildings have been erected in the grounds, but the house
itself contains the library and administrative offices. The original
character of the house with its Italianate-type tower is unspoilt as
are the pretty grounds with little hump-backed bridges over the
stream. The central part of the house was built about 1850 and in
the latter part of the century, it was occupied by Mr Sidney Hill, a
wealthy merchant. He was a great benefactor of the poor of the
neighbourhood and his son Thomas Sidney Hill who succeeded
to the estate in 1908 carried on his good work. At Langford,
Sidney Hill built the Victoria Jubilee Langford Homes in 1890 and
at Churchill, the Wesleyan Cottages in 1907, both for elderly
people. Among the other buildings he erected for public benefit,
was the picturesque clock tower where Front Street and Back
Street (and what more descriptive names could be chosen?) join
at Churchill.

Most of the village of Churchill is near the junction of the A368,
from Weston-super-Mare to Bath, and the A38 from Bristol to
Taunton, for like many villages, there was always the tendency to
move near the main roads. Here are the village shops and some
modern houses among the older properties, but the church and
Churchill Court are a mile or so to the north up the hill. The name
has intrigued many people who asked if it is connected with Sir

Winston Churchill or his ancestors. The name probably means what it says, the "church on the hill", but by a mere accident, certain distant ancestors of Sir Winston once owned Churchill Court. Ralph Jenyns who died in 1572 and his wife are said to be the ancestors of Sarah Jennings who married the first Duke of Marlborough and they are buried in the south aisle of St John's Church at Churchill. Sir John Churchill, a cousin of the Duke, bought the Court in 1652, perhaps because the name of the village was the same as his own. Interesting effigies in the church are those of Sir John and Sarah Latch. Sir John is in a half reclining position, pulling back the shroud from the face of his dead wife. The story goes that Sir John, returning to Upper Langford Court from the Battle of Newbury in 1644, found that his wife had died in childbirth that morning. Beneath are shown their children, seven sons and four daughters and a baby in swaddling clothes who may have been responsible for Sarah's death. Two of the daughters and two of the sons carry skulls to show they were also dead at the time. The church itself is mostly in the Perpendicular style, but has some probable fourteenth-century features. Although today Churchill is a quiet country village within Bristol's commuter area, in the seventeenth and eighteenth centuries, many of its occupants worked as miners winning calamine in the surrounding district for use in Bristol brass foundries.

Sandford, just off the main road from Churchill to Weston-super-Mare, has a number of old houses, probably once occupied by quarry workers engaged in quarrying and mining activities on Sandford Hill, but these are scattered among modern and between-wars houses and bungalows which stretch along the road to Winscombe, or what was once known as Woodborough, for Winscombe itself, with its church, is high on the adjoining hill.

When the Cheddar Valley Railway Line was constructed in 1869, the nearest station to Winscombe was Woodborough on the lower land. It was decided to rename the station Winscombe in order to avoid confusion with another station at Woodborough in Wiltshire. A rather grandiose public house in modern Winscombe is still "The Woodborough" and an office block is known as Woodborough Chambers. Because of the railway, Woodborough developed into present-day Winscombe with its busy shopping centre serving much of the surrounding area and its through road connecting Weston-super-Mare with the A38 at

Sidcot, busy with heavy lorries and traffic. In 1980 local residents resisted Avon's proposals for a bypass, although the parish council approved the proposal to include Winscombe in their structure plan as a shopping, health, social and educational centre for the area. Many of the residents are commuters from Bristol and Weston-super-Mare, as well as people who retired there to be in a lively centre with especially beautiful surroundings, near the coast.

The parish church of St James, high on the hill, is the heart of the old village of Winscombe. The church is famous for its hundred-foot-tall Somerset tower, visible for miles around, and also for its ancient stained-glass windows. The great tower is four stages high and on the west face, on one of the blank windows of the second stage, is a carving of a vase with a lily, the symbol of the Annunciation. The fifteenth-century stained glass is in the north Lady Chapel, where the east window represents St Anthony, the Virgin, the Crucifixion and St John, while the north window shows St Catherine, holding her wheel, the Virgin and St John the Baptist. Another fifteenth-century window is opposite in the south aisle and in the north wall of the chancel is early sixteenth-century glass, with typical yellow silver staining, showing three aspects of St Peter. It is said that there was a lot more ancient glass which was removed by the Victorian restorers. They did, however, insert a lovely east window, tall lancets of glowing colours, reputed to be by William Morris. In the churchyard is an enormous yew tree, believed to be six hundred years old.

Barton Camp at Winscombe provides holidays and outings for about one thousand children each year. The Bristol Children's Help Society built the first dormitory block in 1976-8 and since then, they have provided a sports and study centre and work was proceeding in 1980 on a small-holding. Children from five years of age to eleven are catered for, as well as handicapped youngsters, and they all have a wonderful holiday, made possible by voluntary work and various fund-raising activities.

North-west of Winscombe is Banwell, overlooked by Banwell Castle, a battlemented residence built about 1845. A building of more ancient foundation is Banwell Abbey, a large house which stands close to Banwell's magnificent church. This is said by some to be the site of Banwell's Saxon monastery, given by King Alfred to Bishop Asser of Sherborne in 885. Evidence on this point is lacking, but its position so close to the fifteenth-century church, which could well stand on a site of an earlier foundation, could bring the house within the ancient monastic precincts. We know that Bishop Bekynton of Wells rebuilt a manor house here in the fifteenth century, perhaps incorporating parts of the older structure, that Bishop Godwin spent much of his time there in the following century and that the house was much altered on subsequent occasions. Although the present ornate building owes much to the Victorian Gothic restoration of the 1870s, it certainly seems to incorporate a number of fifteenth-century and possibly fourteenth-century features, and one end, now a separate residence, The Cloisters, includes the fifteenth-century chapel. The archway to the former stables, which are now converted into a dwelling, bears a seventeenth-century date.

The church is in the Perpendicular style, with a great tower over one hundred feet high and striking features of the interior are the lovely rood-screen of 1521 and the fine fifteenth-century stone pulpit, one of several in the district.

Banwell once had its paper mill, but this has gone and what was once the mill pond is now a bowling green. The High Street of Banwell lives up to its name, because it is quite high on the side of the hill, well above the once marshy lowland. Between the main road through the lower part of the village and High Street, are a considerable number of modern houses, which with some individual styling and gardens, fit in quite well with the nineteenth-century atmosphere of High Street, with the village pump set up to celebrate Queen Victoria's Jubilee and give a water supply to the upper part of the village. West of the village is modern housing development on a larger scale, mostly occupied by commuters and retired people who enjoy country living.

Banwell is a centre of prehistoric interest, for higher up the hill to the west is a cave containing bones of extinct animals. In the early nineteenth century, Mr William Beard of Banwell excavated the cave and was delighted to find an enormous quantity of prehistoric animal bones, including cave bear, cave lion, mammoth and woolly rhinoceros. The cave is not open to the public, but much of Banwell's prehistory and history can be studied in the local museum opened in 1980.

Christon is a tiny place on hilly ground facing Crook's Peak, the only peak in the Mendips. The M5 motorway runs through the valley between Christon and the Peak and the continuous hum of traffic can be heard in Christon and other neighbouring villages. Beside the village road at Christon stands the little church of St

Mary the Virgin, an interesting late Norman church with pseudo-
Norman restoration work of the late nineteenth century. The
original Norman work is well worth a visit. In 1844, it was
decided to sell two of the three bells to raise money for church
repairs. One was bought by Bishop Law for use at his summer
residence on Banwell Hill, named The Caves because of the
Banwell Bone Cave in the grounds of the house, but the bell was
restored to the church in 1915. The view of Crook's Peak through
the church porch is very pleasing. The Court adjoining the farm
was almost completely rebuilt in 1822.

South of Christon and close to Avon's southern boundary is
Loxton, like Christon a small rural village, overlooked by Crook's
Peak. The direction signs to Loxton Church are more conspicuous than the church itself, for its squat stuccoed tower is
hidden away under the slope of the hill. The only access is a
footpath which suddenly branches off along the outside of a
farmhouse wall. Like Christon church, St Andrew's Church has a
Norman south doorway. The pulpit is of stone and belongs to
that fine collection of fifteenth-century stone pulpits found in the
area. That at Loxton seems to have been carved out of a single
block of stone. Some of the medieval glass in the church was
discovered some years ago in a box in the hayloft of the old
rectory stables. The Old Rectory was rebuilt in 1884 and adjoins
the road through the village.

Hutton to the north of Loxton lies on a busier highway leading
to Uphill and Weston-super-Mare. The church and the Court
stand on slightly higher ground to the south of the road and
round them a select modern estate has developed of such a
pleasing appearance that few could complain of its proximity to
the ancient buildings. Hutton Court, adjoining the churchyard
with the usual doorway leading from manor to church, is now a
high-class restaurant. Quite a large part of it dates from the
fifteenth century or the early part of the sixteenth century. The
west front was added early in the eighteenth century and other
additions made later, but the house both inside and outside has
the atmosphere of the traditional manor house. The church, on
the other hand, although fifteenth century, was subject to the
usual church alterations and "improvements" of the nineteenth
century, when the south aisle and chancel were added and the
south porch destroyed. It contains late fifteenth- and early sixteenth-century brasses of the Payne family. Together with
Loxton, Christon and Banwell, the village was heavily fined in

Henry III's reign, because of the failure of two men to appear before the Mendip Forest Court for killing a deer. The greatest part of the village lies along the main road and to the north of it where there is a mixture of eighteenth-century and twentieth-century modern houses, for we are approaching Weston-super-Mare now and its outlying suburbs.

South of Hutton and just within the Avon border with Somerset is Bleadon, a picturesque little village and when approached down the hill from the north, there is a fine view of its church and the quarries beyond. The focal point is the small green adjoining the small post office and village shop, with its colourful front garden and the church of St Peter and St Paul behind. On the green is the village cross. It is said that the shaft was removed and placed in the village for hitching horses. In 1929, a new rector decided to recover it and found part supporting a hen roost. It was re-erected on the green and the present head was added. However, the original head may well be a piece of carving incorporated in the right wall of the church porch. The church itself dates from the early fourteenth century with its chancel of this date and the carving in the porch of the latter part of the fourteenth century. Its tower is fifteenth century, but although impressive is not so tall as others in the district. The Perpendicular stone pulpit is of the same type as several others in nearby churches and all these may have been made by the same craftsmen.

Further down the road are two village pumps in a pretty setting in front of two old cottages set at an angle to each other, the Well House, the chief source of water before main water came to the village. They are still in working condition and, we are told, they were used during the severe water shortage caused by the 1976 drought. There is a story that Bleadon derives it name from a particularly bloody battle with the Danes, who tied up their boats at Uphill while raiding the interior. An old woman found the boats and cut them adrift and the local inhabitants killed the Danes at Bleadon as they returned to find their escape cut off. Unfortunately there is no evidence that the story is true. There is practically no modern development at Bleadon, although the old cottages and houses are being restored and converted into pleasant dwellings. It is a charming village built on the most westerly slope of the Mendip Hills as they run down towards Uphill and the sea, to reappear briefly as Brean Down and the islands of Flat and Steep Holm.

10

Weston and the Yeo Moors

Within the southern border of Weston-super-Mare is Uphill on Uphill Pill, which flows into River Axe just before it reaches Weston Bay. Overlooking the village is its Norman church, a coastal landmark, now partly roofless, although occasional services are held there, and the churchyard, perched on the edge of the old quarries, is still used for burials. The church is appropriately dedicated to St Nicholas, the protector of sailors and others. As one might expect, certain gravestones commemorate those who lost their lives by drowning. There is a legend that the inhabitants started to build St Nicholas Church in the village, but the Devil kept moving the stones to the ridge to make it difficult for them to attend services. However, variations of this story are common legends. The tower on the ridge, a little inland from the church, is an old windmill. On the pill below the church, where many small craft are moored, is the old coal wharf and a boat-building and repair yard.

In spite of continuous development from Uphill to Weston-super-Mare, it still retains a village atmosphere. The oldest house is the early seventeenth-century Uphill Farm on the corner of Uphill Road and Uphill Way, where antiques are sold. Uphill Castle or Manor is a large residence at the lower end of Uphill Road with extensive grounds, but it is neither a castle nor a manor house. Built about 1805, it is a castellated building, a reminder of the times when "castles" were built with slate roofs. Over the Bridgwater Road is Devil's Bridge, a railway bridge said to be named after a landowner, "Devil" Payne, who refused to sell his land to the railway unless they provided him with a station. A platform was set up, but it was never agreed that any trains would stop there and Payne is said to have stood on the platform waving his arms and shouting abuses as the unheeding trains went by.

Weston-super-Mare is now far from being a village. It is a flourishing seaside resort visited by tourists from various countries and a particular favourite with Midland people. It is the nearest major seaside resort for Bristol and Bath and during the season there are steady streams of day trippers from these cities. The residents prefer it in the winter months when the crowds have gone and the town turns away from the tourist trade to local life, for it is a lively place with societies and clubs for most interests.

In the early nineteenth century, it was a small fishing village, but the growing interest in sea bathing and the supposed healthy nature of the ozone, produced by the great extent of mud at low tide, attracted many visitors and its village status was at an end. In 1806 Weston was little more than what were known as Watersill Road, West Lane, Bearn Back Road, the Street and Bristol Road, with very few buildings and many fields. By 1821, although it had become a fashionable resort, it still had only 735 inhabitants, including two doctors. Hot and cold baths had been erected on Knightstone, then joined to the shore by a pebble bank, while the beach had three bathing machines, available only, of course, at high tide. There were few amusements, but you could hire a jaunting car, a sedan chair, a pony or a donkey, or collect shells on the beach. Even in those days Weston was relatively accessible from Bristol or Bath, a three-hour journey by coach from Bristol, or five hours from Bath. In those days it was generally the wealthy who patronized such resorts as Weston, but the advent of the railway later in the century brought such pleasures within the reach of the not-so-wealthy. In later years, because it is an easy drive from Bristol, now even easier by the M5 motorway, many of its permanent residents are commuters and retired people who like the sea breezes, although the growing industrial development in the area is providing more local employment. As a result of these pressures, there has been considerable housing development, a process which is still going on rapidly in the North Worle area on Weston's eastern fringe, one of the principal development areas in the Woodspring District.

Although Worle is now within Weston-super-Mare's boundary, it was once a separate village, historically older and much more important than the group of fishermen's cottages which were Weston. In 1822 it was described as three miles and in 1916 as two and a half miles from Weston. The nucleus of the village is still discernible just north of the Bristol road and up the hill round the church, but many of its older buildings are now separated by modern houses. Although the village has changed, its name has remained unaltered since its first mention in Domesday Book.

St Martin's Church was rebuilt in the fifteenth century, but its Norman work is retained in the font, the tower base and south door. Until the Dissolution, the manor belonged to Woodspring Priory and misericords on the north side of the chancel of Worle's church came from that establishment. The brutally murdered Edward Bustle was buried in the churchyard in 1609. His throat had been cut, his legs severed and his body mutilated. His murderers were hung in chains.

West of the church and adjoining the road is a buttressed medieval stone building, now a school but used as a barn in 1822. It was probably a barn connected with the church in medieval times. It is said that at one time Worle villagers did not tolerate the arrival of any member of the legal profession, who would be immediately drummed out of Worle accompanied by beatings and duckings. The origin of this animosity is unknown.

Rising above Worle is Worle or Worlebury Hill where there is a large promontory Iron Age hill fort. It can be approached from Worle, Kewstoke or Weston-super-Mare by pleasant walks through woods. Between 250 B.C. and the Roman invasion, a tribal battle took place here and the slaughtered defenders were buried with the customary offerings of pig in their own granary pits within the fort. Although the numerous half-filled granary pits can be seen, some very close to the footpath, the sword-cut bones recovered from them are in Woodspring Museum in the town.

Iron Age storage pits were not the only pits dug on Worle Hill, for in 1566 a source of calamine, used in brass making, was found there and worked for some time.

On the inland end of Worle Hill is a tower, once a windmill. It was later used as a viewpoint and so gained the name of the Observatory by which it is generally known. It is a conspicuous feature when approaching Weston from Bristol and now contains private dwellings.

Just east of Weston-super-Mare is Locking and, although conspicuous for its RAF Station, Weston's industrial trading estate and housing development, there are still some old houses clustered near the church with an unexpected village character. The church was restored and enlarged in 1814, but retained its fourteenth-century tower and its fascinating Norman font, carved with primitive figures on four corners, with hands outstretched, the arms as long as the legs are short. There is also one of the district's fifteenth-century stone pulpits.

Near the church and close to the Old Coach House Inn, stands the former manor house, now much altered. In 1750, the house had 150 acres of land, but most of this was sold and developed with houses. Even the immediate grounds of the house are now occupied by several superior modern houses and outside the fence of one of these and bordering a drive to another, is a row of standing stones. The house was once occupied by the Reverend Stiverd Jenkins who was so keen on antiquities that he had a stone circle brought from an unknown site on Mendip or an equally elusive site near Glastonbury to decorate his lawn. In 1685, the owner of Locking Manor was John Plumley, who backed the wrong side during the Monmouth Rebellion and was hunted as a traitor. His barking dog gave away his hiding place in a wood near his home and he was hanged from a tree. His distraught wife clasped the dog and threw herself into a well at the back of the house. Her ghost with the dog in her arms was said to have been seen occasionally around the house.

Kewstoke is on the north side of Worle Hill and can be reached either from Worle or along the toll road, a pleasant woodland and coastal drive from Weston-super-Mare, or the energetic could climb Worle Hill from Weston and descend through the woods by the Monks' Steps. Although on the borders of Weston, Kewstoke is still very much a village with only sparse modern building, overlooked by the fifteenth-century tower of its ancient church. During restorations in the mid nineteenth century, a reliquary was found hidden in a concealed recess in the wall of the nave. It held a wooden cup with some dark substance in the bottom, identified as blood sediment. It is believed to have been one of the vessels sold at Canterbury after Thomas à Becket's murder. These contained Canterbury Water, water mixed with some of Becket's blood. It may have been a cherished possession of Woodspring Priory and hidden in Kewstoke church at the Dissolution. These relics are now in Taunton Castle Museum, although the space where they were found is still visible.

Woodspring or Worspring Priory was founded at the beginning of the thirteenth century by William de Curtenai, a grandson of one of the murderers of St Thomas à Becket, but whether in expiation of the crime is uncertain. It was one of the very few Augustinian Victorian houses established in this country, among them the Augustinian Abbey at Bristol, the forerunner of Bristol Cathedral and Keynsham Abbey. It lies near the coast some four miles to the north of Kewstoke and there are splendid views of the Channel from the tower. The Landmark Trust are restoring the monastic buildings and it is possible to visit them by arrangement.

North-east of Kewstoke is Wick St Lawrence, the home of the Wycks whose descendants are buried in Yatton church. As might be expected, Wick's small fifteenth-century church, restored in the nineteenth century and again in the 1970s, is dedicated to St Lawrence. The pride of the church is the beautifully carved stone pulpit which came from Woodspring Priory and is one of the finest in Avon, although it was damaged in a storm, for Knight in his *Seaboard of Mendip* quotes from a report in the *London Chronicle* of 14th January 1791: "Last week at Wick St Lawrence . . . a Thunderbolt struck the Weather Cock . . . entered the West Window . . . and cracked the Pulpit, which was built with Stone." The font is Norman and the porch originally had a priest's room over it, but of this only a window and canopied niche remain. Many people are intrigued by the words "The Providential Deliverance from imminent peril" in the inscription on the north wall of the church in a memorial tablet to the Reverend William Harkness. It refers to his escape from drowning when his horse bolted and dragged his carriage into a pond. The horse was drowned. Across the road from the church is the village cross in a fair state of preservation. It is an Ancient Monument.

Near the village once ran the Weston, Clevedon and Portishead Light Railway, familiarly known as the W.C. and P. among other names. Most people were sorry to see it closed in December 1939, including ourselves as we often watched it trundling along the Gordano Valley. Although we never travelled on it, we have been told that it was an experience not to be forgotten, similar to a journey on *The Titfield Thunderbolt*, filmed elsewhere in our area. The track of the W.C. and P. has now almost entirely disappeared. Much of the metal was taken in the drive for wartime scrap metal for steel processing. A good deal of the railway strip

Village pumps, Bleadon

Uphill and Weston-super-Mare from the old church, Uphill

Old cottages and church, Kewstoke

The leaning tower of Puxton church

Market cross and Ship and Castle Inn, Congresbury

Clifton Foot Harriers at the Old Inn, Congresbury

Family monument in St John's Church, Kenn

Nailsea Town Centre

Broad Street, Wrington

Barrow Gurney, village scene

Dundry village and church tower

Nineteenth-century Parochial School, Long Ashton

Cottages in Old Church Road, Clevedon

Manor House, Clapton-in-Gordano

The Friends' Meeting House, St Mary's Road, Portishead

The village of Pill near the mouth of the River Avon

has been absorbed by adjoining house owners and buildings such as chicken runs have appeared on it. I (Edmund) have acquired a small portion for pipeline laying.

Close to the junction of the Bristol road with the M5 motorway is St Georges, easily missed as the motorway approach rises above the village. From the approach can be seen the Woolpack Inn, named after a wool-packing station which once operated nearby. It was a main road public house *en route* from Bristol to Weston-super-Mare and was a favourite with passing motorists, but like the village it became isolated when the motorway was built and now relies more on local custom and a sporting clientèle.

To the east of St Georges, and reached by a winding minor road is Puxton, on the flat land of Puxton Moor which is continuous with the low-lying land of the Yeo, interspersed with rhynes (pronounced "rheens") or ditches, stretching away to Congresbury. On the edge of the moor is the small church of the Holy Saviour, with its tower leaning at such an acute angle that it looks as if it would fall at any moment, bringing its strange-looking weathercock to the ground. Over the wall of the small churchyard hang branches of apple trees and in the season they are so packed with ripe fruit within easy reach of the ground that we are amazed that they are not raided by all the small boys of the village. Perhaps everybody in Puxton grows apples or perhaps there is a lack of small boys. Perhaps Puxton has always had a plentiful supply of apples for the use of common land was once allocated by drawing a marked apple for each acre of land, after the commoners had been summoned to Puxton church by the bell. Land left over was allotted by an auction method known as the inch of candle. The highest bidder by the time an inch of candle had burned down was the leaseholder. The rent collected was used to defray the costs of the ceremony, including a considerable proportion for food, drink and tobacco for the ensuing revels in which all took part.

The church, itself, has fourteenth and fifteenth-century windows, although the date carved over the porch is 1557, so this is probably the date of a restoration. Inside, the church looks as if it has stood still in time. There are gnarled wooden ancient pews, some old box pews, so high that you could sleep in them without being seen by the rest of the congregation, a high Jacobean pulpit in one corner, a Jacobean reading desk in the other and Jacobean altar rails. Above the pulpit are seen the wooden ends of the old rood-loft and above the reading desk, the damaged wall from which the rood-loft was removed, still remains untouched. Even inside the church, the angle of the tower is clearly visible. I am sure that Sir John Betjeman would include this delightful and homely little church among his Rip Van Winkle churches.

As to the village, it has not entirely stood still, but its twisting lanes and scattered cottages have kept their nostalgic charm for there is little evidence of smart new conversions, however tasteful. In fact, Puxton is a rural surprise, within a few minutes' drive from populous Weston. The village seems hidden away and although the church is clearly seen on the approach from Sandford, the road suddenly twists away as if to pass it by and with the same suddenness swings back again into the village. Now it is the church's turn to be hidden from view, unless you happen to notice the small sign which not too conspicuously points the way.

Across the flat lands bordering the Yeo is Congresbury, standing on the river itself on the A370 from Weston-super-Mare to Bristol, and on an important junction of this road with the B3133 from Yatton. As might be expected, it is a large village, which doubled its population in the 1960s by the building of new housing estates largely inhabited by commuter residents from Bristol and elsewhere.

Congresbury's parish church of St Andrew has a fine spire surmounting its lofty tower. It is a spacious church, built to accommodate a congregation from miles around. There was a great restoration in the fifteenth century, but some thirteenth-century features were retained and there is a fine Norman font encircled round its middle by cable carving and mounted on a thirteenth-century base. An interesting feature is the figures terminating the pendants between the clerestory windows. They appear to have toothache and are thought to commemorate Bishop Bytton of Bath and Wells, who was said to be a great healer, particularly of toothache. Tradition says that the first church, a wattle building, was erected by an early saint, St Congar, who planted his stick to provide shade and the stick turned immediately into a tree. King Ina hearing of this miraculous tree presented land at Congresbury on which to build a stone church and a monastery was established there. The miracle is reminiscent of the Holy Thorn, which sprouted at Glastonbury from Joseph of Arimathea's staff. A tree just east of the church, in the churchyard and bound by an iron hoop, is said to be the legendary tree and earned the name of St Congar's walking stick. Although he died in Jerusalem, St Congar is reputed to have been brought back to Congresbury for burial.

Almost in line with the church and tree and just within the east hedge of the churchyard is a massive pink granite monument, standing on a grey granite base. It commemorates Charles Capel Hardwick of the parish, who died in 1849 and who, in 1830, was wounded by a highwayman, but caught up with his assailant in the centre of the village and handed him over to the law. Hardwick is buried at Hutton.

Adjoining the churchyard is the lawn of the priests' house or refectory, for many years used as the vicarage, an imposing fifteenth-century building, very ecclesiastical in its appearance, with an impressive porch which can be seen between trees from the churchyard. The house was extended about 1824 and now appears in two distinct styles side by side. The newer wing is now the vicarage and the medieval part is used for church functions, such as Sunday morning meetings for children, playgroups and similar activities.

Congresbury seems to have a surprising number of old public houses. There is the "Ship and Castle", almost on the main Bristol road, opposite the splendid village cross. The inn sign shows the Bristol coat of arms, the Ship and the Castle, although it is some miles from the Bristol boundary. Down the road towards Langford is the charming little early eighteenth-century corner inn, once a bakery, "The Plough", so called because it was once a small-holding. Close to the church is the seventeenth-century Old Inn, which was a beerhouse in 1758 and probably long before that. On Wrington Road is the "White Hart", another seventeenth-century building, but much altered and extended, once a farmhouse and brewhouse for Urchinwood Manor.

Near the church is a modern estate for elderly people, neat bungalows round two quadrangles linked by an archway and there is a similar estate in Mill Lane close to Mendip Mills, where small prefabricated buildings are made. The vicar told us that the church is well supported, but as the village is mainly a commuter area, there are frequent changes in the congregation. In fact, he had never known a church with such a large turnover.

There are few places that make cider today, other than the large commercial firms, but at Congresbury, the Richards family have been producing cider since 1974, cider more to the taste of the rural cider drinker and of those who prefer the country type.

Only a mile or so north of Congresbury is Yatton, a village with another large church, with a truncated spire, a conspicuous landmark for some distance around. In recent years, a light and airy chapter house has been added to the side of the church of a design which reflects the truncated spire, but of such modern style that it cannot be confused with the fabric of the ancient church, a refreshing alternative to the pseudo-Gothic of the extensions of the nineteenth century. As to the church itself, although the lower stages of the tower are early thirteenth century and the north and south transepts belong to the latter part of that century, the remainder is mainly of fifteenth-century date.

In the north transept is a fine alabaster tomb of Sir Richard Newton of Court de Wyke, who died in 1449, and his wife. Their effigies lie on the top of the tomb and Sir Richard's head rests on a wheatsheaf, the emblem of the Newtons, and he is in judge's robes. Beyond this tomb is the Newton chapel, an extension of the north transept built by Lady Isobel de Cheddre, wife of Sir John Newton of Court de Wyke who died in 1488. Their joint tomb occupies a deep niche in the wall of the church. Lady Isobel died in 1498 and her wandering ghost is reputed to be seen on Christmas Eve, making her way from the site of Court de Wyke at Claverham, along Well Lane and the Causeway at Yatton to Yatton church for the Midnight Mass. Two other niches in the church contain effigies, believed to be those of Robert de Gyene and his wife Egelina de Wyke.

On the west wall of the church, on either side of the doorway, are statues of St Peter and St Paul of 1708. They were once in Bath Abbey, decorating an organ which was removed to Wells and then to Yatton church. For some years the statues were missing, but finally were found in a nearby house in Yatton and were set up in the church. The organ itself has been very much restored and probably very little of it is original. In part of the east end of the churchyard is the burial ground of a local gypsy family, the Joules, conspicuous by the low oblong iron border that surrounds some of their graves. Just outside the enclosure, one of the Joules headstones has the following epitaph:

Here lies Morily Joules
A beauty bright
That left Isaac Joules
Her heart's delight.

Close to the church is the Old Rectory with its fifteenth-century façade, now used by a firm of building contractors. With windows overlooking the churchyard is the fifteenth-century former Church House, where the "church ales" used to be provided, later used as almshouses and now as private dwellings, but keeping its old name The Church House.

Yatton's economic growth goes back to the middle of the last century when, in 1847, it became an important railway junction with a main line station. The truncated spire of the church still dominates Yatton in spite of the fact that it has grown from a village to the size of a small town and that the population almost doubled between 1970 and 1980. Only ten miles from Bristol, Yatton has become quite a commuter area, although light industry does provide some local employment. Large estates have sprung up around the old village, but further development on any considerable scale is not now contemplated.

Kingston Seymour to the north-west of Yatton lives up to its pretty name, an attractive marshland village of old cottages and houses, with colourful gardens and a sprinkling of well-designed modern houses. A village of the Yeo flats, it is so low-lying that the green sluggish waters of the rhynes adjoin the road, and even the churchyard is bordered by a rhyne within twenty feet of the church of All Saints, making it almost an island. This low-lying land, drained by the rhynes and protected against the sea, only a couple of miles to the west, by sea banks, gives excellent pasturage for dairy cattle, but there have been disasters in past centuries. In the porch of the church is a black framed notice: "On January 20th 1606 and the 4th of James I an inundation of the Sea-water by overflowing and breaking down the Sea-banks happened in this Parish of Kingstone-Seamore and many others adjoining by reason whereof many Persons were drowned and much Cattle and Goods were lost, the water in the church was five feet high and the greatest part lay on the ground about ten days—William Bower". Early in the eighteenth century, another flood destroyed cattle, sheep and corn. The possibility of flood was raised again in 1979 by the National Farmers' Union and it was proposed to improve the defences in 1980, although there was no immediate cause for alarm.

The old spelling in the church of "Seamore" would seem to explain the name of the village, but it is reputed to have derived from a lord of the manor, a member of the Seymour family, who was one of the barons at the signing of the Magna Carta.

To the north-east of Kingston Seymour on the road from Yatton to Clevedon is another moorland settlement, the village of Kenn. The church, the Drum and Monkey Inn and the little post office and general shop form a string along the B3133 road from Clevedon to Yatton. The church of St John the Evangelist is conspicuous for the stepped pyramid stone roof which has been added to the short Norman tower. It is approached from a side road, easy to miss, off the B3133. The chancel is thirteenth century, but most of the remainder of the church was restored in 1861. There are some interesting pieces recovered from the old church, including, from a tomb of the Kenn family, some figures which now occupy a niche over the door to the tower. In this family group, Sir Christopher Kenn, who died in 1593, kneels opposite his two daughters, while his wife, Florence, reclines beneath with a baby and a book. Possibly they may have belonged to the Kenn family who were ancestors of Bishop Thomas Kenn, Bishop of Bath and Wells during the Monmouth Rebellion and one of the seven bishops who refused to publish the "Declaration of Indulgence" reissued by James II. Over the south door is an inscription concerning Sir Nicholas Stalling, who died in 1605 and who married Florence Kenn within nine months of her husband's death.

The "Drum and Monkey", formerly the "Rose and Crown", is an ancient inn and its central part is obviously much older than the side additions. There was once a landlady whom the regulars called "Nellie No-Change" because of her constant habit of having no change about her. So attached was she to the pub that she never really left it. She died after an attack by burglars and is said to have been seen in a black skirt and white apron, while her disembodied voice has been heard singing in the Gents. When "Nellie No-Change" was licensee in the early years of this century, there was a mystery at Kenn. A lady, living with her sister in the village, walked to Clevedon, about two miles away, for some shopping. She was last seen sitting on the parapet of the bridge, singing, about three hundred yards from the "Drum and Monkey". She was never seen again.

In the field behind the "Drum and Monkey", the last public hanging in Somerset took place in 1832. Three local men had fired some stacks of corn because one of them had been fined for selling cider without a licence. The hanging was carried out with great ceremony. The Chief Constable, the High Sheriff, the prison governor, chaplain and magistrates were present with a great number of constables, forming an impressive procession for the occasion, to say nothing of the many sightseers who must have gathered for this exciting spectacle.

From Kenn, a minor road runs south-eastwards across Kenn Moor and then turns north-eastwards to Nailsea, a village which has grown into a town in a remarkably short time. It has not increased by natural expansion, but by a well-defined scheme for a Comprehensive Development Area, planned in stages and continued over a number of years to attract industries, businesses and large-scale housing development, all within easy access of Bristol. The scheme has brought firms from afar, including Marconi Avionics, which supplies equipment for marine oil rigs and aviation. The town centre, with its shops around the pedestrian precincts and other facilities, including its large, light library, is a good example of present-day development and further stages of the Town Centre Plan are still to be completed. It is anticipated that by 1981, the town centre will serve some 175,000 people and that the new industries will provide employment for the skilled and unskilled and for many school leavers, a particular problem at the present time. In spite of all this development, there are still quite a few old buildings, sometimes in incongruous proximity to the new.

Nailsea was famous for its glass making for nearly one hundred years from 1788 until 1873. The site of the glass factory was about a mile out of the village and within a short distance could be obtained all the requirements of the undertaking, clay, sand, lime, coal and building stone. The products were mainly bottles and window glass, but fanciful and colourful objects such as glass walking sticks, rolling pins, miniature furniture, pipes and flasks from the Nailsea works have pride of place in many collections of old glass. Although some of these decorative items were produced commercially, many were the work of apprentices. Wages were high at the Nailsea works and, in spite of the furnace heat, working conditions were comparatively good. Hannah More who did so much work in the education of the poor and who lived in Avon at Cowslip Green and Barley Wood near Wrington, spoke highly of the living standards, praise indeed from Hannah, the "Bishop in petticoats". Coal mining was another of Nailsea's old industries, but coal has not been mined for many years.

Claverham, to the south-west of Nailsea on a minor road to Yatton and less than a mile from the A370 from Bristol to Weston-super-Mare, is one of those villages without a centre and straggles along both sides of the minor road to Yatton. There are a few eighteenth-century houses around the village, including the early eighteenth-century Claverham House, much altered in Victorian times, and the Friends Meeting House of 1729 in Meeting House Lane, now a private residence. Claverham's church on the corner of Jasmine Lane is small and modern.

The tall conspicuous metal chimney in Claverham is that of the old tannery. Tanning started in a barn on the site in 1840. The barn burnt down in 1898 and was replaced by other buildings where the industry continued until the 1914-18 war. Tanning was resumed in 1918, but the buildings were destroyed by a second fire in 1928, causing a hundred people to lose their jobs. The tannery was rebuilt, finally closing in the early 1970s. In recent years the property was used by the Imperial Tobacco Company for tobacco research. The present house and outbuildings are on the original site of the de Wyck Manor house, a name perpetuated by the Court de Wyck school opposite the drive to the old site.

11

Towards Bristol

Less than three miles east of Congresbury is the sizeable village of Wrington, looking more like a small market town, with its wide Broad Street where fairs and markets were once held. During the Middle Ages, the manor of Wrington belonged to Glastonbury Abbey and there was a fine manor house until the middle of the eighteenth century.

The imposing church of All Saints dates from the early fourteenth century and the chancel still remains from that period, but the rest of the church is mostly fifteenth century, including the famous West Tower, over 113 feet high, which inspired Sir Charles Barry to build to the same proportions the Victoria Tower at the Houses of Parliament. There were the usual additions and alterations to the church and the extensive Victorian restoration in 1859.

Two nineteenth-century busts in the south porch, each side of the door to the church, commemorate two Wrington celebrities. The one to the east of the door is that of John Locke, the philosopher, who wrote the famous "Essay concerning the Human Understanding". He was born in a cottage adjoining the churchyard in 1632, during his parents' visit to Wrington. A tablet near the north gate of the churchyard marks the site of his birthplace.

The other bust to the west of the door is that of Hannah More, who is buried in the churchyard with her four sisters. She was born in Fishponds in 1745, but spent much of her life in the Wrington area, firstly at Cowslip Green and later at Barley Wood before retiring to Clifton where she died in 1833. With her sisters,

Hannah did much to provide education and improve the lot of the miners and farm labourers, in spite of considerable opposition, both from employers and those she was trying to help. At that time, many Mendip calamine miners lived in Wrington. The Mendip miners generally had a bad reputation for lawlessness and saw no necessity either for education or religion. Some of the gentry and farmers were no more enlightened and, as employers, deeply resented the meddling, as they saw it, of Hannah More. Even certain of the clergy opposed her, but with extraordinary persistence, she penetrated the hovels, faced irate miners and farmers and gradually won them to her side. She taught miners and their children to read and write, set up friendly societies for women, established schools and brought religion back into their lives. Her wish was that her funeral would be a quiet one, a wish not fulfilled, for as her coffin passed over the route from Clifton, the cortège was joined by great crowds of mourners, the shops closed and the bells tolled. The churchyard was packed with all classes of people from the surrounding district. Inside the church, over the south door, is her memorial tablet.

The main part of Wrington is a conservation area and, driving through the village, one sees but little evidence of modern building, as the new estate is to the north of the village. Some local employment is provided by the light industry at Cox's Green. However, in recent years, because of its proximity to Bristol and Weston-super-Mare, Wrington, and indeed the whole Vale of Wrington, has become increasingly popular with commuters and retired people, a popularity reflected in the prices of property.

North-west of Wrington, on the A370 road from Bristol to Weston-super-Mare, is Cleeve, located by its conspicuous pseudo-Norman church adjoining the road. Around and behind it, the land is flat, but on the opposite side of the road, the ground rises in wooded slopes with the long ravine of Goblin Combe. Near the entrance to the Combe is Cleeve Court, built about 1820 for the Reverend Biddulph, who, true to his time, had anti-quarian interests and so incorporated in his house material from Court de Wyke, mentioned in the last chapter. Whatever one may feel about ancient material being built into later structures, at least in this way it was saved from destruction.

A little over half a mile towards Bristol is Brockley, which, like Cleeve, is a village without a definite form. It follows mostly along the main road with some individual houses and farms approached by country lanes. The church is quite difficult to find, unless you see the signpost pointing to the long drive, leading to both the church and Brockley Court.

Brockley Court, now a home for the elderly, was built in the late seventeenth century by the Pigott family, who owned vast estates in the district, including Weston-super-Mare. They traced their descent from Nicholas and Dorothy Wadham who were founders of Wadham College, Oxford, and their figures, with that of Edward I, are portrayed in the stained glass of about 1830 in the family pew in the church. This was no ordinary pew, but a room from which the family could watch the service with the comfort of their own chairs and a warm fire. Evidence of the original wagon ceiling can still be seen and a churchwarden told us that since that ceiling and one over the nave had been removed because of rot or beetle, exposing the rafters, the church had been appreciably cooler.

The Pigotts had extensive alterations made to the church about 1830 and these were done so well that it is sometimes difficult to tell the new from the old. The stone pulpit is a particularly beautiful one and appears to be of late fourteenth-century date, but may have been recut by the Pigotts. The chancel has thirteenth-century window openings and the stained glass on the south side depicts Edward the Confessor, while St Nicholas, to whom the church is dedicated, is shown on the north side. The font is a fine example of Norman work and the south doorway is also Norman, but lacks the robust appearance of most Norman architecture. It is possible that part of it may have been removed or hidden under the plaster, although the thin shafts and miniature capitals make it unlikely that it had any former grandeur.

The church and the Court make a charming group of buildings and the approach to the church itself takes one back to the days of rural peace. An arched iron gateway leads to a broad path of turf between old stone walls overhung with trees and shrubs. Then the church with its fine Perpendicular west tower comes into view through the foliage. Now the cottages which once clustered round the church are no more and the scattered village has moved to the main road, but from the churchyard a way has been laid into the grounds of the Court to make church attendance easier for the elderly residents.

Behind Brockley Court and attached to it is Court Farm, which, although altered and extended over the centuries, is believed to be considerably older than the mansion. We have pleasant memories of a ploughman's lunch there during 1980, while visiting the flower festival at Brockley, Cleeve, Claverham and Chelvey churches and we were taken round the house which has many fascinating features, although the most unusual, the ancient tall chimney of stone slabs, had been taken down after being judged unsafe.

Back on the A370 road, the next lane on the left brings us to Brockley Hall, another Pigott, or Smyth Pigott, house of the late eighteenth century, with additions made in the 1820s. The Hall and its outbuildings are now converted into flats, the Brockley Hall estate. On the east side of the Bristol Road is Brockley Combe, a lovely drive up through woodlands, so lovely that Coleridge wrote a poem about it, but if today he had "gained the topmost site", he would have found the Bristol Airport at Lulsgate.

The lane past Brockley Hall reaches Chelvey in about a mile, hardly a village, but with a church, a manor house, one or two good houses, a farm and a few buildings. It is far enough away from the main routes to be in complete seclusion. The church of St Bridget has been altered and extended through the ages, like most old churches, as is shown by its south Norman doorway, the Norman, font, the early fourteenth-century chancel and Perpendicular tower. A striking feature of the interior is the great carved wooden Jacobean box pew, the family pew of the Tyntes. Traditionally they owe their name to an ancestor, a young knight who so distinguished himself in 1191 on the battlefield that Richard Coeur de Lion, seeing his prowess and garments stained with enemy blood, awarded him a coat of arms with the motto: "*Tinctus cruore Saracens*") Tinted with Saracen blood". The story goes that it was from this motto that he and the family took their name. Unfortunately we cannot associate the brave young knight with the figure in a surcoat engraved on the floor slab at the east end of the south aisle opposite the family pew, as it is dated to about 1260, but it is probably the earliest engraved grave slab in the county. A number of the old bench pews have been preserved in the church and part of the plaster near the north end of the altar rail has been removed to show part of a wall painting.

From the west wall of the churchyard is a fine view of Chelvey Court, with its baroque porch known as "Solomon's Arch", which Pevsner dates to about 1660. The porch is at the southern end of the building and not in the middle, but there was probably a southern part of the house now lost. In the farmyard adjoining the Court is a large buttressed barn and, although it has all the appearance of a tithe barn, it once belonged to the Court. The house next to the farm is the Old Rectory.

Today, Chelvey is one of the smallest villages in Avon, a rare agricultural village with no modern development and very few inhabitants, but in the seventeenth century, the Court would have been an important manor house with its fine park and swannery, the centre of a considerable estate. The site of the swannery is now occupied by the railway line and the park is no more, but of all the manor houses in Avon there is probably none to surpass Chelvey Court for its romantic stories of secret rooms and hiding places.

Following the A370 road towards Bristol, we soon come to Backwell, whose growth, mainly in the 1950s, incorporated other hamlets such as West Town and it is very much a commuter area for Bristol. From the Bristol Road, the village with its housing estates creeps up Backwell Hill and includes Church Town, where, as one might guess, the church is. Although St Andrew's Church is now some way from the Bristol to Weston-super-Mare road, the road up to the church was once part of the main road between those two towns, before traffic requirements and gradients dictated a new route.

The church is at the centre of the old manor which was divided into two on the death of the Norman Bishop of Coutances. One half was given to the Rodney family and the other half probably to the Le Sore family, but later the Rodneys appear to have acquired the Le Sore half, for they were certainly combined by 1413. The church, of mixed architecture from the thirteenth to seventeenth centuries, except for the Norman font and part of the chancel, contains tombs of the Rodneys, distinguished by the Rodney coat of arms with the three eagles. Sir John Rodney fell in love with a widow, the daughter of Viscount Howard of Bindon. She spurned him for the aged Earl of Hertford and, broken-hearted, he followed her to the inn at Amesbury, locked himself in a room, wrote an 140-verse poem to her in his blood and then killed himself with his sword. The Rodney manor house, near the church, was destroyed by fire, but the Le Sore manor house, Sores Court, although much altered, still stands in a lovely position beneath Backwell Hill. It is approached by the long country lane, Hillside Lane, a pretty walk, although there are now bungalows on one side and at the top of the lane appears the grey-fronted old house with a flight of steps leading down to the gardens. Below the house a footpath leads across the fields to St Andrew's Church. By the church is an old tithe barn and opposite is Court Farm, scheduled as an historic building and once the residence of the manorial bailiffs.

When the glassworks were operating in Nailsea from 1788 to 1873, many of the Backwell inhabitants worked there and in fact two of the owners, J. R. Lucas and Edward Horner, lived at Backwell, Lucas at what is now Backwell Hill House and Horner at West Town House.

Although Backwell is primarily a commuter village, there are still many interesting corners and lanes with eighteenth- and nineteenth-century cottages, some older, and quite a number of fine old houses. There is a new sports centre with swimming-pool to the west of the crossroads and a lively adult education centre, while there is still something of a village atmosphere in the village shops and pubs. Altogether, Backwell is a very pleasant place in which to live.

Within the bounds of Backwell parish is Farleigh, which, like West Town, borders the present main Bristol to Weston-super-Mare road, the A370. In 1267 the Le Sore manor was granted a charter for a weekly market and an annual fair. The fair was held in Farleigh next to the George Inn, which, in the days of coach travel, was a posting station. To this fair many products of the surrounding countryside were brought for sale, including sheep and cattle. The fair was concluded with entertainment, such as wrestling, and in more recent times this was replaced by the usual roundabouts and stalls, but, like many village activities, the fair has disappeared.

A further mile along the A370 road is Flax Bourton, where, above the Norman arch of the south doorway of its church of St Michael and All Angels, is a fine Norman carving showing St Michael slaying a dragon. Opposite was another "angel", for here was the Angel Inn. Due to traffic hazards, however, it is no longer licensed but used as a private residence. In the late eight-eenth century, there lived in Flax Bourton the "Lady of the haystack". A young girl suddenly arrived in the village and made her home in a haystack where she lived for four years, helped and fed by local people who did their best to persuade her to give up this strange way of life. She could not tell who she was or whence she came. Hannah More was one of those who took an interest in

her. When her mental affliction became worse so that she had to
be taken to an asylum, Hannah collected money among the local
ladies and had her sent to a more congenial haven in London. She
died there in 1800. As one might expect, all kinds of romantic
stories were invented about her origin.

There are some interesting old houses in Flax Bourton but very
little modern development around the village itself. Before the
introduction of the strict planning laws which control village
development today, many villages were involved in the break-up
and sale of large estates, but Flax Bourton was not one of these.
Much of the land on the more easily developed levels to the north
of the A370 is part of the Wraxall estate, one of the remaining
extensive estates still intact and consequently much of the land is
still farmed.

South of the A370, on the road linking this and the A38, the
Bristol to Bridgwater road, is Barrow Gurney in a picturesque
setting, close to the three contiguous reservoirs, which, with the
Chew Valley and Blagdon reservoirs, are the main sources of
Bristol's water supply. The Barrow reservoirs were constructed in
1852, 1868 and 1897 and Barrow House, on the site of the old
manor house, was demolished during the construction of the first
one. Two years later, it developed a leak and had to be drained.
This was a disaster because it was then Bristol's main pure water
supply. In 1846, of Bristol and Clifton's 300,000 inhabitants only
5,000 had pure water and the remainder of the population were
dependent on wells, many unfit for use. To make matters worse,
the temporary loss of the reservoir was followed by a serious
drought.

Barrow Gurney at the time of the Domesday Book was known
as Berve and was one of the many properties of the Norman
Bishop of Coutances. It passed by marriage to the de Gournay
family of Harptree and Farrington and after many owners came
into the possession of the Gibbs family during the nineteenth
century. It is a one-road or perhaps a one-lane village and,
although there are several old buildings, its medieval appearance
is deceptive because parts of the village were rebuilt and
extended in the 1920s by Henry Martin Gibbs whose initials
appear over the doorways of some of the houses.

The village does not appear to have a church, but there is the
parish church of St Mary and St Edward, adjoining Barrow
Court, about a mile and three quarters from the village by road,
although there is a footpath. The way lies almost to the A370 and

along a turning to the left, marked to Barrow Court. Although a Tudor building, it was partly rebuilt as a Jacobean house and much restored in the late nineteenth century and the church was rebuilt a little later. The Court and the church stand on the site of an ancient Benedictine nunnery of which there is little trace. For many years, Barrow Court was a Diocesan Training College, but in the 1970s, a scheme was launched to convert the Court and ancillary buildings into a charming residential complex of flats and houses. In the churchyard is a group of graves of the Gibbs family who once lived at the Court.

Southwards along the A38 towards Bridgwater, we pass the Bristol Airport at Lulsgate on the right between Potters Hill and Redhill. The small village of Redhill, with its 1844 church, is just slightly off to the right and a little further on, a lane nearly opposite a motel leads to Cowslip Green, the one-time residence of Hannah More, who is remembered for her work for the education of the poor, and who lies buried in Wrington churchyard. However, in her day, she was better known as an authoress and poetess and to Cowslip Green came many celebrities of the arts, including David Garrick, Dr Johnson, Boswell, Horace Walpole and Reynolds.

To the east of Cowslip Green and to the north of Blagdon Lake is Butcombe, an unspoilt little village, almost lost in the folds of the hills. All the ways to Butcombe from Cowslip Green, from Nempnett Thrubwell or from Redhill, lie along narrow twisting lanes meeting at the bottom of the valley where the ancient Mill Inn stands beside the stream. The cottages and farms climb the steep hill to the little church of St Michael with its decorative south tower. For all its out of the way appearance, Butcombe is known for a local industry, for the Butcombe Brewery, on the scale of the old village breweries, brews a very good Butcombe Ale.

In the same hilly country, a couple of miles along the same twisting lanes to the south-east, is the tiny scattered village of Nempnett Thrubwell. There are a few pleasant old houses, but the most conspicuous building is the church of St Mary with its Perpendicular tower and Norman work in its south doorway. There was once an impressive Neolithic chambered tomb here, but it was opened in 1788 when human bones were found and by the middle of the nineteenth century it had been converted into a limekiln and destroyed. It was known by the romantic name of Fairy Toot and there were stories of fairy music coming from its interior.

Nearer Bristol by a winding lane to the north is Winford. We knew it as a market village and the site of the Winford Orthopaedic Hospital. The hospital is still there, but the cattle market is no longer in the centre of the village and has moved to a site outside on the Chew Magna road. However, if the wind is in the right direction, you can still occasionally hear the monotonous drone of the auctioneer's voice when you stand in the churchyard. In the days of Winford Market, there was always a constant procession of farmers across the road between the market and the Prince of Waterloo public house, probably named after the Duke of Wellington. There is no Winford Market now, but the Avon Livestock Centre, with a large building instead of the temporary hurdles of the old market. The farmer has a longer walk to the pub and where the crowds and animals used to throng on market days, there is now an estate of new houses.

The centre of the village is round the pub and the church of St Mary and St Peter, rebuilt in 1796, but with a tall Perpendicular west tower. Adjoining the churchyard is a grimly romantic-looking building, with great blank walls and small windows. This is Court Farm, with a date of 1593, although parts are said to be medieval and it is believed to have been the manor house. The present Winford Manor is about a mile to the south-west at the top of the steep Parsonage Lane. It was built as their new residence by the previous occupants of the manor in the seventeenth century. The other side of the crossroads is the Rectory, an exceptionally fine Queen Anne house with a beautiful shell hood.

Before about 1850, teasels were grown at Winford, Dundry, Blagdon, Harptrees and elsewhere for carding or combing wool in the Yorkshire mills. The ripe heads were cut and bundled, dried in the open air and graded into "kings", "middlings" and "scrub". The journey by cart to Bradford and back took about three weeks. Woad is known to have grown near Winford during the eighteenth century and later. The leaves were cut, pulped, made into balls and dried to make indigo blue for the dyers. Iron ore was once worked on a small scale at Winford, but in later years, the Winford Red Company worked ochre deposits for use in paints.

The Orthopaedic Hospital was built 1928-30, although, like most hospitals, it has considerably increased in size since then and it has a very fine reputation. From the village, the buildings are quite inconspicuous and except for a modest directional sign at the beginning of the road to Barrow Gurney, you would not suspect its existence.

Although away from the main road, Winford still retains its rural character. It is a growing village, within easy commuting distance of Bristol and a fair amount of modern development has taken place, especially on the old market site. No doubt the proximity of the Avon Livestock Centre with easy communication for local farmers will help Winford to retain its status as an agricultural centre.

Bristol Airport's principal runway runs from east to west and is in a direct line with Winford. It cannot be extended westwards because of the fall of the land and any extension would be eastwards across the A38 road, bringing the airport and runway nearer the village. Proposals for such an extension are under review to accommodate larger aircraft and longer flights. The estimated cost of the project is between nine and twelve and a half million pounds, and three alternatives have been suggested: lowering the A38 road and extending the runway over it, rerouting the A38 into Felton Common, and making an alternative route for the A38 round Felton Common. As might be expected, the Winford Parish Council have raised objections to the scheme which would probably be completed by the end of 1983 on the grounds of added noise and the spoliation of Felton Common by the erection of numerous landing lights, some of them forty feet high. The matter will probably have to be decided at a public inquiry.

The most familiar landmark on the ridge of hills to the south west of Bristol is the tall tower of Dundry church. From Dundry Hill came some of the stone for buildings in the city and the evidence is left in the pock-marked surface of part of the plateau. Over this ridge the old Bristol Road still makes its way to Wells, the main route before the present A37 road was made. Visitors to Bristol undergoing the ordeal of a carriage ride down the precipitous Dundry hill at least had a magnificent view of the city, as have those who drive down today.

The church, as befits its siting, is dedicated to St Michael. Rebuilt in 1861, the church has retained its remarkable fifteenth-century tower, nearly one hundred feet high with a most elaborate crown with ornate pinnacles and parapet. The Merchant Venturers of Bristol erected the tower in the fifteenth century to guide their seamen and today it is visible for many miles around. Like the similar tower of St Stephen's Church in Bristol, it belongs to the group of Somerset towers, which include several in the southern part of Avon. In the churchyard close to the old village cross is the Dole Stone, where money used to be "doled" out to the poor. On its hill-top position, still difficult of access in icy weather, Dundry has not been overtaken by the Bristol suburbs which have extended along the lower slopes. Although there are some new houses, there are still a good number of old stone-built cottages and the school with its belfry. It is still mainly a one-street village, lined with grey stone buildings.

Down the hill to the A38 and a mile towards Bristol, a minor road leads to the left to the A370 and the very different village of Long Ashton, just outside the Bristol boundary. The oldest part of the village is near the church, but, for the most part, Long Ashton was a lineal village with old buildings lining both sides of the road, once the turnpike road. Before the bypass was constructed in the 1960s, the road through the village was the main road to Weston-super-Mare and one of the busiest out of the city. Even now, the village is by no means a backwater, for behind the older houses are considerable modern estates, those on the north side climbing steeply up the hill towards Failand, while those to the south occupy a gentle slope towards the railway and the bypass and there is a fair-size shopping centre to serve the growing population.

Long Ashton was an estate village of Ashton Court, where the Smyth family lived for some four hundred years and, as an estate village at the gates of the Court, it was protected against the urban sprawl and industrialization of the nineteenth and early twentieth centuries. During the rundown of many large estates between the wars, the Smyth fortunes diminished and in 1959, the Bristol City Council purchased the parkland for a public open space and the Court which they are restoring as a centre for conferences and functions.

It is recorded that the Angel Inn, fronting the main road, was given in 1495 by Sir John Choke, then Lord of the Manor, to the village as a Church House, on condition that the inhabitants prayed for his soul for evermore. By 1720, and possibly for some time before that date, the building was also known as "The Angel", perhaps because of its old connection with the parish church of All Saints. At the side of the Angel Inn, Church Lane leads down to the church, passing the tiny Long Ashton Parochial School, with its red pantile roof and double pointed

Gothic-style windows. A stone tablet over the doorway gives its date as 1818.

The spacious late fourteenth-century church of All Saints has many monuments to the lords of the manor, including the colourful tomb, adorned with a great company of angels, of Sir Richard Choke in his robes of office as Lord Chief Justice of England. He died in 1486. As one might expect, there are many memorials to the Smyth family. In the churchyard, leaning against the wall adjoining the doorway leading to the vicarage, is an intriguing epitaph.

The first line is now obliterated, but reads:

Reader who comes to see
My mouldering clay
Know that a fellow apprentice
Took my life away
In bloom of Youth
Ere Nature's glass was ran
I fell a victim
To the Rage of Man.

Another by the path leading to the north door reads:

Grieve not for me my parents dear
I am not dead but sleeping here
My wedding bed is in the dust
Christ is my bride in whom I trust
        M   H
Now, dressed in snowy robes of white
She joins the shining band above
And sings with wonder and delight
The praises of redeeming love

Opposite the church are several of the oldest cottages in the village, some probably medieval. One of these has a Tudor fireplace, a modern addition at the time. Adjoining the church is the pretty Georgian farmhouse and in the farmyard is the fifteenth-century Abbot's barn, but with a modern roof following a fire. The whole group makes a charming cluster of buildings round the medieval church. Church Lane, itself, ends in a farm gate, giving a fine view across the fields of the Victorian Gothic gatehouse leading into the park of Ashton Court.

In past years local employment was found on the Ashton Court estate and on the local farms and market gardens. Iron was won in the Providence area, but like the local coal, this has not been worked for many years. Now some of the residents work in the local Barrow Hospital or in the Long Ashton Research Station, where research is carried out on apples and cider and other fruits and their products, but the majority work in Bristol. However, Mr Wynne Wilson of Long Ashton told us that, in spite of the proximity of the city and the doubling of the population since 1960, both the older and the newer residents enter very much into village life. The fact that Long Ashton has over forty local organizations and clubs is some indication of its independence.

12

The Failand Ridge and the Gordano Valley

On high ground, above the bank of the Avon, is Abbots Leigh, separated from the river by Leigh Woods, which with their varied foliage cover the south side of the Avon Gorge. The name means the Abbot's meadow, for the manor once belonged to St Augustine's Abbey at Bristol and the manor house is said to have been used as a rest house for the canons. Abbots Pool, not far from the George Inn, is believed to have been one of several in that area used for the canons' supply of fish. Today, the Pool is remarkably beautiful and unspoilt in its woodland setting.

The George Inn, named after George III, was probably first licensed in 1790, but like a number of public houses, it was once the Church House. It had stables for the horses of those visiting the church and the church ales were brewed there. Behind the church is a large ornate house known as The Priory, once the dwelling of a single family, but now divided into several parts.

So near Bristol and yet so free from modern housing estates, Abbots Leigh is a highly desirable place in which to live and the few new houses are scattered on the outskirts of the village, with large gardens, often half hidden by woodland and are generally occupied by professional and business people. The older houses and cottages which once housed farm workers are converted and often similarly occupied. The heart of the village is Church Road, opposite the George Inn. Here is the village hall, where we attended a Christmas Fair and were struck by the intimate village atmosphere. Everybody knew everybody and seemed delighted to do so. There are a variety of dwellings in Church Road from cottages to rather grand old houses. The road leads to a small green with the village primary school and Holy Trinity Church, rebuilt in 1848 after a fire which left only the tower, the chancel, the walls of the south arcade and the south doorway. In 1843, part of one of the tower pinnacles and the weathercock were brought down by a storm and in 1831 the church was damaged by lightning.

In spite of its hazardous career, the church still contains the tomb of Sir George Norton, who died in 1815, and his wife. Sir George lived at nearby Leigh Court, where he sheltered the future Charles II after the Battle of Worcester. Disguised as a servant under the name of Will Jackson, Charles arrived at Leigh Court riding behind Jane Lane, Mrs Norton's cousin. The Nortons gladly received them, although they did not realize the identity of the servant. However, the butler recognized the Prince and when some soldiers searched the Court, passed him off as a kitchen boy. For his hospitality, George Norton was awarded his knighthood when Charles became King of England. The present Leigh Court is not the one in which Charles stayed, for it was pulled down in 1811 and the present house built, not quite on the same site, in 1814. This house has also been graced by royalty for Prince Edward, later Edward VII, was entertained there by the then owner, Sir Philip Miles, in 1884. The house, with its great classical-style portico, is now a hospital.

Failand, two or three miles to the south-west of Abbots Leigh, is a scattered village, divided into Upper and Lower Failand. The former is on the Failand ridge centred round the B3128 Bristol to Clevedon Road and the B3129 Leigh Woods to Flax Bourton crossroads, while Lower Failand consists of the church, the village school and a few scattered houses. The modern development is mainly contained within a triangle of roads in Upper Failand, enclosing what was known as Sixty Acres. Development started there between the wars, with the erection of wartime structures, converted to dwellings, set in large gardens. Some of these have been enlarged and modernized but most have been demolished and replaced by estates of superior houses.

Close to the crossroads which forms one angle of Sixty Acres is Longwood House which was originally built as a lunatic asylum by French prisoners of the Napoleonic Wars. They were marched there every day from Stapleton in Bristol. In 1851, it had thirty-nine occupants, including the physician and sixteen staff. Today it comprises several residences.

The Failand Inn was built in 1860 and replaced Ye Olde Fayland

Inn, now used for farming purposes, but once also the magistrates' courthouse. Behind the present inn, in a quarry, is an open-air sidearms shooting range. Further along the Clevedon road and on the opposite side to the Failand Inn, is Plantation Works which makes concrete blocks and slabs. Opposite the inn and adjoining Failand Hill is Failand Lodge, which, according to Mrs Bowden's *Further Findings of Failand*, was built in 1788 as a Court of Justice, but rebuilt in 1839. Failand House, near the bottom of the hill before turning for the village school and church, was built about 1720 by Abraham Elton and extended by Sir Edward Fry who purchased it in 1874. The Fry family were Quakers, descendants of Elizabeth Fry, prison reformer. They were founders of the chocolate and cocoa manufacturing business, now part of the Cadbury-Schweppes combine. Sir Edward and Lady Mirabella Fry, with their daughter Agnes, are buried in the Failands churchyard.

Close to the small village school in Lower Failand is St Bartholomew's Church with its tower and broach spire. The church was built in 1887 at the instigation of Richard Vaughan, whose memorial is in the church, and presented by him to the Rector of Wraxall to administer for the people of Failand.

The Failand ridge was once a lonely desolate place, a haunt of highwaymen. It is now extensively farmed and much of it is part of the Wraxall estate. Although the newcomers are mostly Bristol commuters and although the village has two distinct parts, the population is well integrated, an important factor being the village school which serves both Upper and Lower Failand and is a unifying force in the community.

To the west and at the foot of the ridge overlooking the Nailsea lowlands is Wraxall, centred round what was once the ancient village elm. It was quite a feature of the village, but unfortunately died a few years ago and has been replaced by a young tree, appearing a miniature compared with the compass of the stone base which surrounded the old tree and originally supported the village cross. In recent years, Wraxall has almost joined with the north-eastern development of Nailsea, but still keeps its identity and has very little modern development.

All Saints' Church stands high above the road with its tidy churchyard occupying two levels, each with its own churchyard cross, although the one nearest the church is the old one and is of fifteenth-century date. The south door is Norman with an Early English outer porch doorway, but although most of the church is in the Perpendicular style, much of it was restored in 1851 and again in 1893. Some of the former lords of the manor, the Gorges, are buried within the church and there is the fine tomb chest of Sir Edmund, who died in 1512, and Lady Gorges.

There is a story that George IV visited Wraxall when a boy and was criticized by the rector for playing fives against the tower. It was a common practice to play fives against church walls and many British churches still have the remains of hinge supports for shutters to protect windows against the stray ball. A member of the family with whom the young George is said to have stayed, the Bampfyldes of the mid seventeenth-century Wraxall Court, close to the church, was peculiarly sensitive to the sound of the bells. Sir Charles Warwick Bampfylde is said to have planted trees on the side of the churchyard opposite his house to muffle the sound of the bells and on one occasion cut the bell ropes with a carving knife. For this offence he had to do penance, wearing a white sheet, in front of the congregation, during a service.

In the churchyard behind the church is the old church school, built in 1809, now used chiefly as a store-room. The present school can be seen from the churchyard on the other side of the main road. It is said that the white cottage, Church Lodge, at one of the entrances to the churchyard, was once the schoolmaster's house. It is now the verger's residence and, although Tudor in appearance, was built in 1823 as part of a gift to the church.

The large house at Wraxall is Tyntesfield, the home of Lord Wraxall, well hidden within its park. It is a large, imposing, neo-Gothic building with tall chimneys, tourelles and miniature spires, built about 1820 and considerably enlarged in 1862-4. The existence of the Wraxall estate with its park, farms and lands has helped a great deal to maintain the rural nature of this area today.

Another interesting house is Birdcombe Court or Tower House, which gives its name to Tower House Lane, a steep lane with various drives leading off to secluded houses in woodland settings. The house itself obviously owes its name to its tower. It is a fascinating medieval house and a part could be as old as the thirteenth century. There is a good view of the house from the other side of the valley, where we once helped with the excavation of a Roman villa. We used to look across the little Land Yeo river at the grand tower and the bull pen where the farmer then living at Tower House kept his enormous bull.

Tickenham is reached through Nailsea and is a village of ancient ribbon development along the B3130 to Clevedon, its growth limited by the hillside on the north and low-lying levels on the south. It is in fact a combination of three hamlets, West End, Middletown and Stone Batch. As so often is the case, the church and the Court are a little distance off the main road and on a knoll overlooking the lowlands. The church has the unfamiliar dedication of St Quiricus and St Julietta. There are only two other similar dedications in the country, one in Devon and one in Cornwall. Mother and son were martyred early in the fourth century for their Christian beliefs. In France, St Quiricus is known as St Cyr, in Scotland as Cyrus and in Wales as Curig. It is a change to come across a church where Perpendicular rebuilding has not overlaid most of the characteristics of the older church. It has retained its eleventh-century chancel arch and much of the structure belongs to the twelfth and fourteenth centuries.

Above the churchyard wall can be seen the roofs of Tickenham Court, an old house with two surprising features, a hall dating from about 1400 and a solar wing of about 1500. An interesting resident of Tickenham Court, in the latter part of the seventeenth century, was Eleanor Glanville, a very eccentric lady. She collected butterflies and not only butterflies, but flies and creepy-crawlies and even probed about in cowpats in pursuit of her quarry, not at all usual for a seventeenth-century lady of the manor. In fact, one butterfly, the Glanville Fritillary, which now seems to be confined mostly to the Isle of Wight, was named after her. From the surviving accounts, it would appear that she may have been a little mad. If these accounts are true, then a woman who arranges chairs to whip saying she is riding to Bristol, gives a dinner party on her "wedding day" because she is marrying her son, turns out the miller in the middle of the night and wants to take the mill wheel up to her house, and wanders abroad at all hours of the day and night almost unclothed, might be rather more than eccentric. In fact, the terms of her will were disputed on the grounds of insanity.

On the Channel coast to the west of Tickenham is Clevedon. In 1801 it was a village with 334 inhabitants, but now it is a coastal town with large Victorian grey limestone houses and extensive modern development, housing a population of about 16,000. Up to about 1950, the population increase was due largely to those seeking a quiet seaside town for retirement, but it was augmented very considerably by Bristol commuter residents when car travel between home and work became popular. There are shopping centres in the Triangle and in Hill Road in the upper part of the town, away from the beach, and the large shopping areas of Bristol and Weston-super-Mare are a mere twelve miles or so away, both short journeys on the M5 motorway.

In the summer season, Clevedon does not attract huge crowds as does Weston-super-Mare with its pier and other amusements and with numerous cafés and restaurants, except for the relatively small area at the Marine Lake and miniature railway, it is on the whole more a residential than a holiday town, although it offers the visitor a reasonably quiet stay with pleasant Channel views and cliff walks. Its slender, delicately proportioned Victorian pier is no longer accessible, for part of it collapsed under test in 1970. Now its terminal pavilion stands out at sea as a forlorn metal island where the gulls have taken over. There are hopes that the pier will eventually be restored, but finance is the problem.

The Clevedon sea front is attractive with mid-Victorian and various coloured Regency stucco-fronted houses, so different from the limestone grey of the higher parts of the town. Before the promenade was built, boats used to be drawn up under or between the houses through arches which still exist, although these and the land behind them are not used for fishermen's boats today, but for motor vehicles.

There are some quaint cottages, some thatched in Old Church Road, near the Norman church of St Andrew. Many of the buildings in this road have been removed and those that remain are interspersed with modern houses. There is a small combined general shop and post office adorned with stone carvings, capitals and pilasters in Victorian Gothic taste, which although in proportion to the size of the shop, would be more appropriate on a grand building. At the end of Old Church Road and beside Wain Hill is a pleasant little inlet where a few boats are still to be seen.

Although St Andrew's Church is basically Norman, the nave was pulled down and rebuilt in 1291 and the squat Norman tower was heightened in the seventeenth century by the addition of a further stage. The porch was built in the fourteenth century and there was considerable restoration in the fifteenth, nineteenth and early twentieth centuries, but many of the early features remain.

In the south transept there are particularly sad memorials as they record the deaths of so many young people. There is the Hallam memorial to Henry Hallam and three of his children who died young, Arthur Henry who died at Vienna aged twenty-three years, Eleanor twenty-one years and a younger brother who died in Siena at twenty-six years. There is also a memorial tablet to Abraham and Charles Elton, two children of Clevedon Court, who were cut off by the tide on Birnbeck Island, Weston-super-Mare and drowned in 1819. Arthur Henry Hallam was a great friend of Lord Tennyson, who wrote his famous poem "In Memoriam" when Arthur died in 1833. Victorian development in other parts of the town led to the erection of more conveniently sited churches, but the Old Church, as it is now called, is still a popular place of worship.

Although one might expect to find the manor house near the Old Church, Clevedon Court is two miles away on the east side of the town. This may have been because the intervening land was once liable to flooding, or because the site was more convenient for the administration of the estate. Although the lords of the manor provided their own chapel at the Court, the Old Church remained the burial place for the family. Clevedon Court was built about 1320, altered and enlarged about 1570, with further alterations in the eighteenth and nineteenth centuries, particularly to the west front. The house contains some interesting items collected by the Eltons, who lived in the house from 1709 when it was purchased by Abraham Elton, a wealthy Bristol merchant, until 1973 when it was taken over by the National Trust.

Clevedon Court and Clevedon may well be described as a resort of poets and writers. Sir Charles Abraham Elton, the father of the two boys drowned at Weston, was a poet and writer. Tennyson stayed at the Court when he made his pilgrimage to Arthur Hallam's tomb in 1850. A frequent visitor in Sir Charles's time was William Makepeace Thackeray, who did some of his writing at the Court, including part of *Henry Esmond*. Samuel Taylor Coleridge spent his honeymoon in Clevedon in 1795, although which cottage he rented is in doubt.

An interesting Victorian building of Clevedon is the Market Hall of 1869 which, in recent years, has become rather dilapidated. It was originally built for market gardeners who had previously depended on hawking but later it became a brewery, then an aircraft component factory and lastly a warehouse and light engineering works. Its restoration for use as an arts and crafts centre is under consideration but, here again, finance is a problem.

On the hill to the north of Clevedon is Walton Castle close to

Ladye Bay. Although it looks like an ancient fortress, it was built early in the seventeenth century by the first Lord Poulett. An empty shell for many years, it is now being converted into a private residence.

From the north-east of Clevedon, two ranges of low hills fan out like an elongated V, the northern one ending at Portishead and the southern one merging into the Failand ridge. Between the two lies the Gordano Valley, extending as far as the southern bank of the River Avon at Pill. The middle of this long valley was once marshland, now drained by rhynes to form rich pasture, while on the slightly higher ground at the foot of the hills are a number of villages bearing the name of the valley, Walton-in-Gordano, Weston-in-Gordano, Clapton-in-Gordano and Easton-in-Gordano. The upper slopes of the hills are mostly wooded, while the lower slopes are used for fruit and vegetable growing, particularly the south-facing slopes of the northern range. Occasionally quarries scar the hills. The M5 motorway travels high on its supports and embankments above the valley floor until it hugs the flank of the southern range which it cuts across near Clevedon. The origin of the name "Gordano" is a mystery. One suggestion is that it comes from the Saxon *gara* or *gone* and "dene" meaning a wedge-shaped valley, which certainly describes the valley, but there are other theories.

The first village from Clevedon is Walton-in-Gordano, a small village where the cottages and house are scattered in a woodland setting. The original settlement was near the castle and later became Old Walton. The shift of the village eastward may have been due to an extension of the castle parkland. The church was left behind and eventually fell into ruins until it was finally rebuilt in 1870, when Old Walton had become the Walton Park suburb of Clevedon. To serve the present village, a second church was built in 1839.

Some two miles further along the B3124 Clevedon to Portishead road is Weston-in-Gordano, a long, narrow village on both sides of the road, its development restricted on one side by the hill and on the other by the low-lying land of the valley, stretching away towards the motorway with its glint of cars as they speed towards Bristol or Weston-super-Mare. There are some new houses opposite the church, but on the whole the village seems to have changed but little over the years. The church of St Peter and St Paul adjoins the road, with its fine tower of late thirteenth- or early fourteenth-century date. It has several interesting features, such as the gallery over the south doorway to the nave with a staircase from the porch, ancient roughly hewn benches with poppy-head ends and two sets of choir stalls with curious misericords, carved brackets often seen in cathedrals and larger churches but rarely in simple village churches. For this reason it has been suggested that they may have come from a larger establishment once in the area. The colourful monument of Richard Percyvale, who died in the fifteenth century, is strikingly ornate, but was much restored in the seventeenth century.

The Percivals occupied the manor house, now demolished, for centuries and a box tomb in the churchyard, near the south porch, is said to be that of a crusader ancestor. It is said to be part of a more elaborate monument which once had an honourable position in the church. Is this really the tomb of the crusading Percyvale, who in Richard I's time is believed to have gone on fighting on horseback after a leg and an arm had been hacked off and miraculously lived to return to Weston-in-Gordano to be finally buried there? Needless to say, the story has often been challenged.

The churchyard cross was given in 1910-11 by two sisters, descendants of the Percyvales, in memory of their grandfather, Spencer Percival, the British Prime Minister who was assassinated in the lobby of the House of Commons on 11th May 1812. He insisted on attending the House, in spite of a dream which foretold the actual event, and met his death there as the dream prophesied.

On the other side of the Gordano valley is Clapton-in-Gordano, on the narrow road leading beneath the southern range of hills to Clevedon. Across the intervening flats, Walton-in-Gordano and Weston-in-Gordano can be seen nestling against the northern hillsides. The valley bottom with its drainage ditches is known as Walton Moor, Weston Moor and Clapton Moor, according to the name of the nearest village.

Clapton-in-Gordano has its centre around the road junction near the Black Horse Inn, but half a mile along the narrow lane is the manor house and the church. At a higher level and parallel with the lane, the M5 motorway makes its way south, passing over the hill by a deep cutting which can be seen as a gap in the ridge for many miles.

Almost adjoining the motorway, the church of St Michael is sited, as befits its name, on a grass mound above the Court. The little church is of considerable interest, with its Norman doorway, thirteenth- and fourteenth-century work and with perhaps the oldest benches in the district, said to be as old as the early fourteenth century. Even older is the reputedly thirteenth-century screen, transferred from the Court to the church in the nineteenth century and one of the earliest examples of English domestic screen carving. The most striking monument is that of Edmund Wynter, son and heir of the Wynter family who owned the Court. He died in 1672 and his two sorrowing parents kneel either side of a prayer desk, while underneath sits their child, holding a skull as a symbol of his death.

Adjoining the foot of the church mound is the manor house, Clapton Court, first built in the early fourteenth century by the Arthur family. Richard Arthur made certain additions, including the porch tower, in the middle of the fifteenth century, and over the porch entrance he installed the combined arms of himself and his wife, who was a Berkeley. The last of the Arthurs at Clapton Court was Edward, whose daughter and heiress married into the Wynter family. Subsequently the Court passed to other owners and the usual additions and alterations were made to the building during the eighteenth and nineteenth centuries. The fourteenth-century work has long been demolished and of the fifteenth-century work, only the tower porch and part of the adjoining walling remain.

The Black Horse Inn in the present village centre, half a mile eastwards, is said to date back to the fourteenth century and is that great rarity, an inn with a true rural character. The inn sign shows a black horse and a man in stocks. It appears to represent two aspects of the inn's history, for it was once the village lock-up and the black horse is said to be a reminder of the days when coal, from nearby mines on Clapton Hill, was carried on pack-horse through the village to Portishead for shipment to Wales. Iron was also worked on a small scale, but today, the rural character of Clapton gives no indication of its former industries. Around the inn, clusters the old village with the stone and brick schoolhouse and quaint cottages climbing the narrow lanes. So near Bristol, the inn is a great attraction for weekend visitors and the unspoilt village is a favourite residential place. Further along the lanes and on the main road to Portishead a number of modern houses and bungalows have been built, but there are no estates, the motor-way is up out of sight and sound and only the cars at weekends detract from the village peace.

Across the now drained marshland to the northern end of the

Gordano Valley is Portishead, hardly a village, but a small town. Almost all that is left of the old village is the parish church, the adjoining Court and a few old houses in their vicinity and scattered here and there about the town. St Peter's Church has interesting fourteenth- , fifteenth- and sixteenth-century features and a Norman font, but was much restored and extended in the 1870s. The sixteenth-century Court, with its polygonal corner tower, head-moulded windows and pink brick and stone walling, with the great barn adjoining, makes a picturesque group of buildings. Near the junction of the Bristol and Clevedon roads is the sixteenth-century Grange, another impressive house, once moated and incorporating parts of a much older building. It was probably the old manor house of North Weston, but, like the Court, its extensive estate fell to the inroads of later development. In nearby St Mary's Well Road, set at right angles to the road, is a long, low, thatched cottage, with additions, known as the Friends' Meeting House. In the seventeenth century, this cottage was the home of a Quaker family, who held meetings there, and the building became the Meeting House of the local Quaker community.

Portishead once had its mills and the High Street was known as Mill Street. One of the old mills is now an inn, the "White Lion" at the north end of High Street, and a millstone has been incorporated into its wall. There was another mill at the south end of High Street near the Grange. The pill, which provided water power for the early milling industry and transport for its products, was later converted, at its seaward end, into a dock, in 1879. The dock is still in use for local industry, but the greater traffic goes to the docks seen across the estuary, the Royal Portbury Dock and Avonmouth Docks. Among goods which once came into the Portishead Dock were fuel for the power stations, built in 1929 and 1959, wood pulp from Scandinavia and chemical products. Another industry of Portishead was the universal supply of horseshoe nails, but with the falling demand, the industry turned to screw manufacture.

The construction of the dock halted Portishead's development as a select holiday resort for the gentry, but a few fine villas and the Royal Pier Hotel built in 1830 bear witness to its popularity in the early nineteenth century. However, the coming of the railway brought the trippers, an esplanade was built in 1898 and unemployed men from Bristol were engaged to dig out the area for the construction of the Marine Lake in 1910. An open-air swimming pool now completes the amenities. With its fine Channel views, cliff walks and above all, proximity to Bristol, Portishead has always attracted visitors and between the wars many Bristolians owned weekend chalets on the cliffs. The M5 motorway has made access to Bristol even easier and large estates have grown up in recent years, housing not only retired people and those engaged in local industry, but a great number of Bristol commuters. The population in 1800 was about 200 and today numbers over 10,000.

To the east of Portishead and close to the M5 motorway is the small village of Portbury, housing a good-size commuter population who work in Portishead, Avonmouth and Bristol. In fact the old village has been engulfed by housing estates with views across the lowland of the wide end of the Gordano Valley to the Severn. The M5 service station area is near the village and the motorway runs at a lower level to the north. An obvious sound to the visitor is the continuous hum of traffic, but no doubt residents' ears have become accustomed to it and in some places it is muffled by trees and banks.

The church of St Mary is isolated from the village down a narrow road which is cut off just past the church by the construction of the M5 motorway. The church has some fine Norman work in the south doorway and chancel arch and a Norman font. Of outstanding interest is the chancel chapel on the north side of the church, with its fine vaulted roof. Some of the gravestones in the churchyard are among the oldest in the country dating back to the beginning of the seventeenth century, but much older is the gravestone in the church to William Godwin, dated 1584, for this was part of the High Altar removed at the Reformation. In the village, on the corner of Station Road and Caswell Lane, is the Old Priory, now used as a residence. Its history is rather obscure and it is believed not to have been a priory, but an Augustinian manor house.

A short distance to the north-east of Portbury is Easton-in-Gordano, the last of the four Gordano villages. Very much a built-up area, it is a commuter village for Bristol and the home of some of the Pill boatmen. St George's Church was rebuilt in 1872 and the lower part of the tower, said to be fourteenth century, is all that remains of the earlier church. The churchyard has been the burial place of many seamen and pilots, for it also served the neighbouring village of Pill. Among the pilots buried there was one Cullimore who, in 1775, while out in the Bristol Channel, decided to scale the cliffs of Steep Holm, one of the two mid-channel islands, in search of gulls' eggs, and fell.

Easton-in-Gordano is continuous with the village of Pill, or Crockerne Pill to give it its full name, which is located, as its name implies, round a creek or pill of the River Avon. Here have lived for generations the Pill pilots whose job it is to guide vessels up the Bristol Channel. In past times, the occupation was usually handed down from father to son and, as Pill records show, boys were apprenticed, often at the age of nine, to relatives and the apprenticeship lasted twelve years. Their pilot cutters were small sailing vessels and the pill was their traditional mooring place. The last sailing cutter was replaced by a motor cutter in 1922 and the old vessel is now in the Exeter Maritime Museum.

The pill is an interesting place, even picturesque when the tide is in and the boats ride on the brown water, but when the tide is out, the picture is marred by the great expanse of Avon mud, except to those who have eyes to see beauty in the contours of the glistening mud and in the angles of the boats tilted on the steep sides of the pill. A hundred yards or so away, the pill joins the River Avon and there was once a ferry between the village and Shirehampton on the opposite bank, but this ceased to operate in 1970.

This book started where the River Avon enters the county and we are now at the western end of the Avon Valley, where the river leaves Avon to merge with the Bristol Channel.

Bibliography

Abram, L., *The Old Church of St. Nicholas, Uphill*, L. Abram, 1962.

Archer, Derek (ed.), *Thornbury*, Bailey and Sons, Dursley, 1977.

Atthill, Robin, *Old Mendip*, David and Charles, 1964.

Automobile Association, *Treasures of Britain*, Drive Publications, 1968.

Banks, R.F., *English Villages*, Batsford, 1963.

Barnes, Max, *Bristol A-Z*, Bristol Evening Post (no date).

Barnes, Max, *West Country A-Z*, Bristol United Press, 1971.

Bonham Carter, Victor, *The English Village*, Penguin 1952.

Bonington, M. L., *Long Ashton, Our Village*, Bonington, 1980.

Bowden, L. E., *Further Findings of Failand*, Bowden (no date).

Braine, A., *The History of Kingswood Forest, 1891*. Republished by Kingsmead, 1969.

Brown, Dorothy, *Avon Heritage, the North, the Vale and the Forest*, Bristol Visual and Environmental Group, 1980.

Buchanan, Angus and Neil Cossons, *Industrial Archaeology of the Bristol Region*, David and Charles, 1969.

Cooke, Robert, *West Country Houses*, 1957.

Cossons, Neil, *Industrial Monuments in the Mendip, South Cotswold and Bristol Region*, Bristol Archaeological Research Group, 1967.

Couzens, P. A., *A Companion into the Southwolds*, Couzens (no date).

Couzens, P. A., *The Sodburys*, Bailey and Sons, 1977.

Couzens, P. A., *Southwolds*, Couzens, 1978.

Coysh, W., Mason E. J. and Waite V., *The Mendips*, Robert Hale 1977.

Davis, Graham, *The Langtons of Newton Park*, Davis (no date).

Day, Joan, *Bristol Brass, the History of the Industry*, David and Charles, 1973.

Dunning, Robert, *Somerset and Avon*, Bartholomew, 1980.

Elliott, C. H. B., *Winterbourne*, 1899. Republished by Kingsmead, 1936.

Forrest, Denys, *The Making of a Manor, the Story of Tickenham Court*, Moonraker Press, 1975.

Haddon, John, *Portrait of Avon*, Robert Hale, 1981.

Hobbs, A. J. H., *History of the Parish of Winford*, Hobbs (no date).

Hutton, Edward, *Highways and Byways in Gloucestershire*, Macmillan, 1936.

Hutton, Edward, *Highways and Byways in Somerset*, Chapman and Hall, 1955.

Jordan, Christopher, *Olveston Methodist Church*, Jordan, 1979.

Jordan, Christopher, *Severn Enterprise*. Arthur H. Stockwell, 1977.

Jordan, Christopher, *Severnside Memories*, Jordan, 1979.

Knight, F. A., *The Heart of Mendip*, Dent, 1915. Reprinted by Chatford House Press Ltd. 1971.

Knight, F. A., *The Seaboard of Mendip*, Dent, 1902.

Leech, Roger, *Small Mediaeval Towns in Avon*, Committee for Rescue Archaeology in Avon, Gloucestershire and Somerset, 1975.

Little, Bryan, *Portrait of Somerset*, Robert Hale, 1969.

Marshfield Women's Institute, *Marshfield, Southern Cotswolds*, Marshfield Women's Institute, 1972.

Mee, Arthur, *Gloucestershire*, Hodder and Stoughton, 1966.

Mee, Arthur, *Somerset*, Hodder and Stoughton, 1968.

Muir, Richard, *The English Village*, Thames and Hudson, 1980.

Newman, Paul, *Channel Passage*, Kingsmead, 1976.

Painter, C. H., *A Short History of Hanham*, Painter, 1975.

Pearce, L. C., *The Story of Backwell*, Pearce. (no date).

Pevsner, Nikolaus, *Buildings of England: North Somerset and Bristol*, Penguin, 1958.

Rich, J., *New Dock at Pill*, The Crockerne Pill and District History Society, 1978.

Robinson, W. J., *West Country Churches*, Vol. 1-4, Bristol Times and Mirror, 1914-16.

Robinson, W. J., *West Country Manors*, St Stephen's Press, 1930.

Ryder, T. A., *Portrait of Gloucestershire*, Robert Hale, 1972.

Sims, Percy, *A History of Saltford Village*, Sims, 1976.

Skinner, John, *Journal of a Somerset Rector, 1803-1834*, Edited by H. and P. Coombs, Kingsmead, 1971.

Smith B. and Ralph, E. *A History of Bristol and Gloucestershire*, Darwen Finlayson, 1972.

Verey, D., ed. N. Pevsner *The Buildings of England, Gloucestershire: The Cotswolds*, Penguin, 1970.

Verey, D. ed. N. Pevsner *The Buildings of England. Gloucestershire: the Vale and the Forest of Dean*, Penguin, 1970.

Wadmore, J. A., *Collections for a Parochial History of Barrow Gurney*. Somersetshire Archaeological and N. H. Society, 1897.

West, A. and D. Verey, *Gloucestershire, a Shell Guide*, Faber, 1952.

Whitlock, Ralph, *Somerset*, Batsford, 1975.

Proceedings of the Somersetshire Archaeological and Natural History Society.

Transactions of the Bristol and Gloucestershire Archaeological Society.

Wrington Village Records, University of Bristol, 1969.

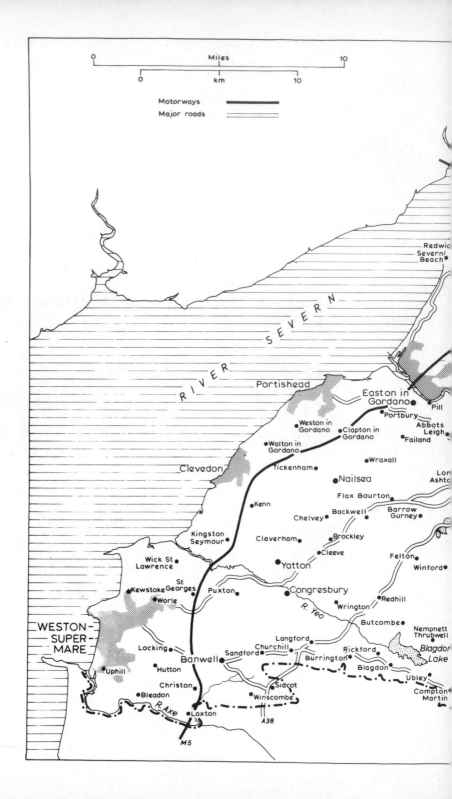

Based upon the Ordnance Survey map with the permission of the Controller of Her Majesty's Stationary Office. Crown Copyright Reserved.

Index